An Essay Upon Projects

Daniel Defoe

16

EasyRead Large

ReadHowYouWant Classics Library

Set in 16 pt. Verdana

TABLE OF CONTENTS

INTORDUCTION

Defoe's "Essay on Projects" was the first volume he published, and no great writer ever published a first book more characteristic in expression of his tone of thought. It is practical in the highest degree, while running over with fresh speculation that seeks everywhere the well-being of society by growth of material and moral power. There is a wonderful fertility of mind, and almost whimsical precision of detail, with good sense and good humour to form the groundwork of a happy English style. Defoe in this book ran again and again into sound suggestions that first came to be realised long after he was dead. Upon one subject, indeed, the education of women, we have only just now caught him up. Defoe wrote the book in 1692 or 1693, when his age was a year or two over thirty, and he published it in 1697.

Defoe was the son of James Foe, of St. Giles's, Cripplegate, whose family had owned grazing land in the country, and who himself throve as a meat salesman in London. James Foe went to Cripplegate Church, where the minister was Dr. Annesley. But in 1662, a year after the birth of Daniel Foe, Dr. Annesley was one of the three thousand clergymen who were driven out of their benefices by the Act of Uniformity. James Foe was then one of the congregation that followed him into exile, and looked up to him as spiritual guide when he was able to open a meeting-house in Little St. Helen's. Thus Daniel Foe, not yet De Foe, was trained under the influence of Dr. Annesley, and by his advice sent to the Academy at Newington Green, where Charles Morton, a good Oxford scholar, trained young men for the pulpits of the Nonconformists. In later days, when driven to America by the persecution of opinion, Morton became Vice- President of Harvard College. Charles Morton sought to include in his teaching at Newington Green a training in such knowledge of current history as would show his boys the origin and meaning of the controversies of the day in which, as men, they might hereafter take their part. He took pains, also, to train them in the use of English. "We were not," Defoe said afterwards, "destitute of language, but we were made masters of English; and more of us excelled in that particular than of any school at that time."

Daniel Foe did not pass on into the ministry for which he had been trained. He said afterwards, in his "Review," "It was my disaster first to be set apart for, and then to be set apart from, the honour of that sacred employ." At the age of about nineteen he went into business as a hose factor in Freeman's Court, Cornhill. He may have bought succession to a business, or sought to make one in a way of life that required no capital. He acted simply as broker between the manufacturer and the retailer. He remained at the business in Freeman's Court for seven years, subject to political distractions. In 1683, still in the reign of Charles the Second, Daniel Foe, aged twenty-two, published a pamphlet called "Presbytery

Roughdrawn." Charles died on the 6th of February, 1685. On the 14th of the next June the Duke of Monmouth landed at Lyme with eighty-three followers, hoping that Englishmen enough would flock about his standard to overthrow the Government of James the Second, for whose exclusion, as a Roman Catholic, from the succession to the throne there had been so long a struggle in his brother's reign. Daniel Foe took leave of absence from his business in Freeman's Court, joined Monmouth, and shared the defeat at Sedgmoor on the 6th of July. Judge Jeffreys then made progress through the West, and Daniel Foe escaped from his clutches. On the 15th of July Monmouth was executed. Daniel Foe found it convenient at that time to pay personal attention to some business affairs in Spain. His name suggests an English reading of a Spanish name, Foa, and more than once in his life there are indications of friends in Spain about whom we know nothing. Daniel Foe went to Spain in the time of danger to his life, for taking part in the rebellion of the Duke of Monmouth, and when he came back he wrote himself De Foe. He may have heard pedigree discussed among his Spanish friends; he may have wished to avoid drawing attention to a name entered under the letter F in a list of rebels. He may have played on the distinction between himself and his father, still living, that one was Mr. Foe, the other Mr. D. Foe. He may have meant to write much, and wishing to be a friend to his country, meant also to deprive punsters of the opportunity of calling him a

Foe. Whatever his chief reason for the change, we may be sure that it was practical.

In April, 1687, James the Second issued a Declaration for Liberty of Conscience in England, by which he suspended penal laws against all Roman Catholics and Nonconformists, and dispensed with oaths and tests established by the law. This was a stretch of the king's prerogative that produced results immediately welcome to the Nonconformists, who sent up addresses of thanks. Defoe saw clearly that a king who is thanked for overruling an unwelcome law has the whole point conceded to him of right to overrule the law. In that sense he wrote, "A Letter containing some Reflections on His Majesty's Declaration for Liberty of Conscience," to warn the Nonconformists of the great mistake into which some were falling. "Was ever anything," he asked afterwards, "more absurd than this conduct of King James and his party, in wheedling the Dissenters; giving them liberty of conscience by his own arbitrary dispensing authority, and his expecting they should be content with their religious liberty at the price of the Constitution?" In the letter itself he pointed out that "the king's suspending of laws strikes at the root of this whole Government, and subverts it quite. The Lords and Commons have such a share in it, that no law can be either made, repealed, or, which is all one, suspended, but by their consent."

In January, 1688, Defoe having inherited the freedom of the City of London, took it up, and signed his name in the Chamberlain's book, on the 26th of that month, without the "de," "Daniel Foe." On the 5th of November, 1688, there was another landing, that of William of Orange, in Torbay, which threatened the government of James the Second. Defoe again rode out, met the army of William at Henley-on-Thames, and joined its second line as a volunteer. He was present when it was resolved, on the 13th of February, 1689, that the flight of James had been an abdication; and he was one of the mounted citizens who formed a guard of honour when William and Mary paid their first visit to Guildhall.

Defoe was at this time twenty-eight years old, married, and living in a house at Tooting, where he had also been active in foundation of a chapel. From hose factor he had become merchant adventurer in trade with Spain, and is said by one writer of his time to have been a "civet-cat merchant." Failing then in some venture in 1692, he became bankrupt, and had one vindictive creditor who, according to the law of those days, had power to shut him in prison, and destroy all power of recovering his loss and putting himself straight with the world. Until his other creditors had conquered that one enemy, and could give him freedom to earn money again and pay his debts— when that time came he proved his sense of honesty to much larger than the letter of the law—Defoe left London for Bristol, and there kept out of the way of arrest. He was visible only on Sunday, and known, therefore, as "the Sunday Gentleman."

His lodging was at the Red Lion Inn, in Castle Street. The house, no longer an inn, still stands, as numbers 80 and 81 in that street. There Defoe wrote this Essay on Projects." He was there until 1694, when he received offers that would have settled him prosperously in business at Cadiz, but he held by his country. The cheek on free action was removed, and the Government received with favour a project of his, which is not included in the Essay, "for raising money to supply the occasions of the war then newly begun." He had also a project for the raising of money to supply his own occasions by the establishment of pantile works, which proved successful. Defoe could not be idle. In a desert island he would, like his Robinson Crusoe, have spent time, not in lamentation, but in steady work to get away.

H. M.

AUTHOR'S PREFACE

TO DALBY THOMAS, ESQ., One of the Commission's for Managing His majesty's Duties on Glass, &c

***

SIR,

This Preface comes directed to you, not as commissioner, under whom I have the honour to serve his Majesty, nor as a friend, though I have great obligations of that sort also, but as the most proper judge of the subjects treated of, and more capable than the greatest part of mankind to distinguish and understand them.

Books are useful only to such whose genius are suitable to the subject of them; and to dedicate a book of projects to a person who had never concerned himself to think that way would be like music to one that has no ear.

And yet your having a capacity to judge of these things no way brings you under the despicable title of a projector, any more than knowing the practices and subtleties of wicked men makes a man guilty of their crimes.

The several chapters of this book are the results of particular thoughts occasioned by conversing with the public affairs during the present war with France. The losses and casualties which attend all trading nations in the world, when involved in so cruel a war as this, have reached us all, and I am none of the least sufferers; if this has put me, as well as others, on inventions and projects, so much the subject of this book, it is no more than a proof of the reason I give for the general projecting humour of the nation.

One unhappiness I lie under in the following book, viz.: That having kept the greatest part of it by me for near five years, several of the thoughts seem to be hit by other hands, and some by the public, which turns the tables upon me, as if I had borrowed from them.

As particularly that of the seamen, which you know well I had contrived long before the Act for registering seamen was proposed. And that of educating women, which I think myself bound to declare, was formed long before the book called "Advice to the Ladies" was made public; and yet I do not write this to magnify my own invention, but to acquit myself from grafting on other people's thoughts. If I have trespassed upon any person in the world, it is upon yourself, from whom I had some of the notions about county banks, and factories for goods, in the chapter of banks; and yet I do not think that my proposal for the women or the seamen clashes at all, either with that book, or the public method of registering seamen.

I have been told since this was done that my proposal for a commission of inquiries into bankrupt estates is borrowed from the Dutch; if there is anything like it among the Dutch, it is more than ever I knew, or know yet; but if so, I hope it is no objection against our having the same here, especially if it be true that it would be so publicly beneficial as is expressed.

What is said of friendly societies, I think no man will dispute with me, since one has met with so much success already in the practice of it. I mean the Friendly Society for Widows, of which you have been pleased to be a governor.

Friendly societies are very extensive, and, as I have hinted, might be carried on to many particulars. I have omitted one which was mentioned in discourse with yourself, where a hundred tradesmen, all of several trades, agree together to buy whatever they want of one another, and nowhere else, prices and payments to be settled among themselves; whereby every man is sure to have ninety-nine customers, and can never want a trade; and I could have filled up the book with instances of like nature, but I never designed to fire the reader with particulars.

The proposal of the pension office you will soon see offered to the public as an attempt for the relief of the poor; which, if it meets with encouragement, will every way answer all the great things I have said of it.

I had wrote a great many sheets about the coin, about bringing in plate to the Mint, and about our standard; but so many great heads being upon it, with some of whom my opinion does not agree, I would not adventure to appear in print upon that subject.

Ways and means also I have laid by on the same score: only adhering to this one point, that be it by taxing the wares they sell, be it by taxing them in stock, be it by composition – which, by the way, I believe is the best – be it by what way soever the Parliament please, the retailers are the men who seem to call upon us to be taxed; if not by their own extraordinary good circumstances, though that might bear it, yet by the contrary in all other degrees of the kingdom.

Besides, the retailers are the only men who could pay it with least damage, because it is in their power to levy it again upon their customers in the prices of their goods, and is no more than paying a higher rent for their shops.

The retailers of manufactures, especially so far as relates to the inland trade, have never been taxed yet, and their wealth or number is not easily calculated. Trade and land has been handled roughly enough, and these are the men who now lie as a reserve to carry on the burden of the war.

These are the men who, were the land tax collected as it should be, ought to pay the king more than that whole Bill ever produced; and yet these are the men who, I think I may venture to say, do not pay a twentieth part in that Bill.

Should the king appoint a survey over the assessors, and indict all those who were found faulty, allowing a reward to any discoverer of an assessment made lower than the literal sense of the Act implies, what a register of frauds and connivances would be found out!

In a general tax, if any should be excused, it should be the poor, who are not able to pay, or at least are pinched in the necessary parts of life by paying. And yet here a poor labourer, who works for twelve pence or eighteen pence a day, does not drink a pot of beer but pays the king a tenth part for excise; and really pays more to the king's taxes in a year than a country shopkeeper, who is alderman of the town, worth perhaps two or three thousand pounds, brews his own beer, pays no excise, and in the land-tax is rated it may be at 100 pounds, and pays 1 pound 4s. per annum, but ought, if the Act were put in due execution, to pay 36 pounds per annum to the king.

If I were to be asked how I would remedy this, I would answer, it should be by some method in which every man may be taxed in the due proportion to his estate, and the Act put in execution, according to the true intent and meaning of it, in order to which a commission of assessment should be granted to twelve men, such as his Majesty should be well satisfied of, who should go through the whole kingdom, three in a body, and should make a new assessment of personal estates, not to meddle with land.

To these assessors should all the old rates, parish books, poor rates, and highway rates, also be delivered; and upon due inquiry to be made into the manner of living, and reputed wealth of the people, the stock or personal estate of every man should be assessed, without connivance; and he who is reputed to be worth a thousand pounds should be taxed at a thousand pounds, and so on; and he who was an overgrown rich tradesman of twenty or thirty thousand pounds estate should be taxed so, and plain English and plain dealing be practised indifferently throughout the kingdom; tradesmen and landed men should have neighbours' fare, as we call it, and a rich man should not be passed by when a poor man pays.

We read of the inhabitants of Constantinople, that they suffered their city to be lost for want of contributing in time for its defence, and pleaded poverty to their generous emperor when he went from house to house to persuade them; and yet when the Turks took it, the prodigious immense wealth they found in it, made them wonder at the sordid temper of the citizens.

England (with due exceptions to the Parliament, and the freedom wherewith they have given to the public charge) is much like Constantinople; we are involved in a dangerous, a chargeable, but withal a most just and necessary war, and the richest and moneyed men in the kingdom plead poverty; and the French, or King James, or the devil may come for them, if they can but conceal their estates from the public notice, and get the assessors to tax them at an under rate.

These are the men this commission would discover; and here they should find men taxed at 500 pounds stock who are worth 20,000 pounds. Here they should find a certain rich man near Hackney rated today in the tax-book at 1,000 pounds stock, and tomorrow offering 27,000 pounds for an estate.

Here they should find Sir J– perhaps taxed to the king at 5,000 pounds stock, perhaps not so much, whose cash no man can guess at; and multitudes of instances I could give by name without wrong to the gentlemen.

And, not to run on in particulars, I affirm that in the land-tax ten certain gentlemen in London put together did not pay for half so much personal estate, called stock, as the poorest of them is reputed really to possess.

I do not inquire at whose door this fraud must lie; it is none of my business.

I wish they would search into it whose power can punish it. But this, with submission, I presume to say: The king is thereby defrauded and horribly abused, the true intent and meaning of Acts of Parliament evaded, the nation involved in debt by fatal deficiencies and interests, fellow-subjects abused, and new inventions for taxes occasioned.

The last chapter in this book is a proposal about entering all the seamen in England into the king's pay – a subject which deserves to be enlarged into a book itself; and I have a little volume of calculations and particulars by me on that head, but I thought them too long to publish. In short, I am persuaded, was that method proposed to those gentlemen to whom such things belong, the greatest sum of money might be raised by it, with the least injury to those who pay it, that ever was or will be during the war.

Projectors, they say, are generally to be taken with allowance of one-half at least; they always have their mouths full of millions, and talk big of their own proposals. And therefore I have not exposed the vast sums my calculations amount to; but I venture to say I could procure a farm on such a proposal as this at three millions per annum, and give very good security for payment – such an opinion I have of the value of such a method; and when that is done, the nation would get three more by paying it, which is very strange, but might easily be made out.

In the chapter of academies I have ventured to reprove the vicious custom of swearing. I shall make no apology for the fact, for no man ought to be ashamed of exposing what all men ought to be ashamed of practising. But methinks I stand corrected by my own laws a little, in forcing the reader to repeat some of the worst of our vulgar imprecations, in reading my thoughts against it; to which, however, I have this to reply:

First, I did not find it easy to express what I mean without putting down the very words – at least, not so as to be very intelligible.

Secondly, why should words repeated only to expose the vice, taint the reader more than a sermon preached against lewdness should the assembly? – for of necessity it leads the hearer to the thoughts of the fact. But the morality of every action lies in the end; and if the reader by ill-use renders himself guilty of the fact in reading, which I designed to expose by writing, the fault is his, not mine.

I have endeavoured everywhere in this book to be as concise as possible, except where calculations obliged me to be particular; and having avoided impertinence in the book, I would avoid it too, in the preface, and therefore shall break off with subscribing myself,

Sir,
Your most obliged, humble servant
D. F.

AUTHOR'S INTRODUCTION

Necessity, which is allowed to be the mother of invention, has so violently agitated the wits of men at this time that it seems not at all improper, by way of distinction, to call it the Projecting Age. For though in times of war and public confusions the like humour of invention has seemed to stir, yet, without being partial to the present, it is, I think, no injury to say the past ages have never come up to the degree of projecting and inventing, as it refers to matters of negotiation and methods of civil polity, which we see this age arrived to.

Nor is it a hard matter to assign probable causes of the perfection in this modern art. I am not of their melancholy opinion who ascribe it to the general poverty of the nation, since I believe it is easy to prove the nation itself, taking it as one general stock, is not at all diminished or impoverished by this long, this chargeable war, but, on the contrary, was never richer since it was inhabited.

Nor am I absolutely of the opinion that we are so happy as to be wiser in this age than our forefathers; though at the same time I must own some parts of knowledge in science as well as art have received improvements in this age altogether concealed from the former.

The art of war, which I take to be the highest perfection of human knowledge, is a sufficient proof of what I say, especially in conducting armies and in offensive engines. Witness the now ways of rallies, fougades, entrenchments, attacks, lodgments, and a long et cetera of new inventions which want names, practised in sieges and encampments; witness the new forts of bombs and unheard-of mortars, of seven to ten ton weight, with which our fleets, standing two or three miles off at sea, can imitate God Almighty Himself and rain fire and brimstone out of heaven, as it were, upon towns built on the firm land; witness also our new-invented child of hell, the machine which carries thunder, lightning, and earthquakes in its bowels, and tears up the most impregnable fortification.

But if I would search for a cause from whence it comes to pass that this age swarms with such a multitude of projectors more than usual, who – besides the innumerable conceptions, which die in the bringing forth, and (like abortions of the brain) only come into the air and dissolve – do really every day produce new contrivances, engines, and projects to get money, never before thought of; if, I say, I would examine whence this comes to pass, it must be thus:

The losses and depredations which this war brought with it at first were exceeding many, suffered chiefly by the ill-conduct of merchants themselves, who did not apprehend the danger to be really what it was: for before our Admiralty could possibly settle convoys, cruisers, and stations for men-of-war all over the world, the French covered the sea with their privateers and took an incredible number of our ships. I have heard the loss computed, by those who pretended they were able to guess, at above fifteen millions of pounds sterling, in ships and goods, in the first two or three years of the war – a sum which, if put into French, would make such a rumbling sound of great numbers as would fright a weak accountant out of his belief, being no less than one hundred and ninety millions of livres. The weight of this loss fell chiefly on the trading part of the nation, and, amongst them, on the merchants; and amongst them, again, upon the most refined capacities, as the insurers, And an incredible number of the best merchants in the kingdom sunk under the load, as may appear a little by a Bill which once passed the House of Commons for the relief of merchant-insurers, who had suffered by the war with France. If a great many fell, much greater were the number of those who felt a sensible ebb of their fortunes, and with difficulty bore up under the loss of great part of their estates. These, prompted by necessity, rack their wits for new contrivances, new inventions, new trades, stocks, projects, and anything to retrieve the desperate credit of their fortunes. That this is probable to be the cause will appear further thus. France (though I do not believe all the great outcries we make of their misery and distress – if one-half of which be true, they are certainly the best subjects in the world) yet without question has felt its share of the losses and damages of the war; but the poverty there falling chiefly on the poorer sort of people, they have not been so fruitful in inventions and practices of this nature, their genius being quite of another strain. As for the gentry and more capable sort, the first thing a Frenchman flies to in his distress is the army; and he seldom comes back from thence to get an estate by painful industry, but either has his brains knocked out or makes his fortune there.

If industry be in any business rewarded with success it is in the merchandising part of the world, who indeed may more truly be said to live by their wits than any people whatsoever. All foreign negotiation, though to some it is a plain road by the help of custom, yet is in its beginning all project, contrivance, and invention. Every new voyage the merchant contrives is a project; and ships are sent from port to port, as markets and merchandises differ, by the help of strange and universal intelligence – wherein some are so exquisite, so swift, and so exact, that a merchant sitting at home in his counting-house at once converses with all parts of the known world. This and travel make a true-bred merchant the most intelligent man in the world, and consequently the most capable, when urged by necessity, to contrive new ways to live. And from hence, I humbly conceive, may very properly be derived the projects, so much the subject of the present discourse. And to this sort of men it is easy to trace the original of banks, stocks, stock-jobbing, assurances, friendly societies, lotteries, and the like.

To this may be added the long annual inquiry in the House of Commons for ways and means, which has been a particular movement to set all the heads of the nation at work; and I appeal, with submission, to the gentlemen of that honourable House, if the greatest part of all the ways and means out of the common road of land taxes, polls, and the like, have not been handed to them from the merchant, and in a great measure paid by them too.

However, I offer this but as an essay at the original of this prevailing humour of the people; and as it is probable, so it is also possible to be otherwise, which I submit to future demonstration.

Of the several ways this faculty of projecting have exerted itself, and of the various methods, as the genius of the authors has inclined, I have been a diligent observer and, in most, an unconcerned spectator, and perhaps have some advantage from thence more easily to discover the faux pas of the actors. If I have given an essay towards anything new, or made discovery to advantage of any contrivance now on foot, all men are at the liberty to make use of the improvement; if any fraud is discovered, as now practised, it is without any particular reflection upon parties or persons.

Projects of the nature I treat about are doubtless in general of public advantage, as they tend to improvement of trade, and employment of the poor, and the circulation and increase of the public stock of the kingdom; but this is supposed of such as are built on the honest basis of ingenuity and improvement, in which, though I will allow the author to aim primarily at his own advantage, yet with the circumstances of public benefit added.

Wherefore it is necessary to distinguish among the projects of the present times between the honest and the dishonest.

There are, and that too many, fair pretences of fine discoveries, new inventions, engines, and I know not what, which – being advanced in notion, and talked up to great things to be performed when such and such sums of money shall be advanced, and such and such engines are made – have raised the fancies of credulous people to such a height that, merely on the shadow of expectation, they have formed companies, chose committees, appointed officers, shares, and books, raised great stocks, and cried up an empty notion to that degree that people have been betrayed to part with their money for shares in a new nothing; and when the inventors have carried on the jest till they have sold all their own interest, they leave the cloud to vanish of itself, and the poor purchasers to quarrel with one another, and go to law about settlements, transferrings, and some bone or other thrown among them by the subtlety of the author to lay the blame of the miscarriage upon themselves. Thus the shares at first begin to fall by degrees, and happy is he that sells in time; till, like brass money, it will go at last for nothing at all. So have I seen shares in joint-stocks, patents, engines, and undertakings, blown up by the air of great words, and the name of some man of credit concerned, to 100 pounds for a five-hundredth part or share (some more), and at last dwindle away till it has been stock-jobbed down to 10 pounds, 12 pounds, 9 pounds, 8 pounds a share, and at last no buyer (that is, in short, the fine new word for nothing-worth), and many families ruined by the purchase. If I should name linen manufactures, saltpetre-works, copper mines, diving engines, dipping, and the like, for instances of this, I should, I believe, do no wrong to truth, or to some persons too visibly guilty.

I might go on upon this subject to expose the frauds and tricks of stockjobbers, engineers, patentees, committees, with those Exchange mountebanks we very properly call brokers, but I have not gaul enough for such a work; but as a general rule of caution to those who would not be tricked out of their estates by such pretenders to new inventions, let them observe that all such people who may be suspected of design have assuredly this in their proposal: your money to the author must go before the experiment. And here I could give a very diverting history of a patent-monger whose cully was nobody but myself, but I refer it to another occasion.

But this is no reason why invention upon honest foundations and to fair purposes should not be encouraged; no, nor why the author of any such fair contrivances should not reap the harvest of his own ingenuity. Our Acts of Parliament for granting patents to first inventors for fourteen years is a sufficient acknowledgment of the due regard which ought to be had to such as find out anything which may be of public advantage; new discoveries in trade, in arts and mysteries, of manufacturing goods, or improvement of land, are without question of as great benefit as any discoveries made in the works of nature by all the academies and royal societies in the world.

There is, it is true, a great difference between new inventions and projects, between improvement of manufactures or lands (which tend to the immediate benefit of the public, and employing of the poor), and projects framed by subtle heads with a sort of a deceptio visus and legerdemain, to bring people to run needless and unusual hazards: I grant it, and give a due preference to the first. And yet success has so sanctified some of those other sorts of projects that it would be a kind of blasphemy against fortune to disallow them. Witness Sir William Phips's voyage to the wreck; it was a mere project; a lottery of a hundred thousand to one odds; a hazard which, if it had failed, everybody would have been ashamed to have owned themselves concerned in; a voyage that would have been as much ridiculed as Don Quixote's adventure upon the windmill. Bless us! that folks should go three thousand miles to angle in the open sea for pieces of eight! Why, they would have made ballads of it, and the merchants would have said of every unlikely adventure, "It, was like Phips's wreck-voyage." But it had success, and who reflects upon the project?

> "Nothing's so partial as the laws of fate,
> Erecting blockheads to suppress the great.
> Sir Francis Drake the Spanish plate-fleet won;
> He had been a pirate if he had got none.
> Sir Walter Raleigh strove, but missed the plate,
> And therefore died a traitor to the State.
> Endeavour bears a value more or less,
> Just as 'tis recommended by success:
> The lucky coxcomb ev'ry man will prize,
> And prosp'rous actions always pass for wise."

However, this sort of projects comes under no reflection as to their honesty, save that there is a kind of honesty a man owes to himself and to his family that prohibits him throwing away his estate in impracticable, improbable adventures; but still some hit, even of the most unlikely, of which this was one of Sir William Phips, who brought home a cargo of silver of near 200,000 pounds sterling, in pieces of eight, fished up out of the open sea, remote from any shore, from an old Spanish ship which had been sunk above forty years.

THE HISTORY OF PROJECTS.

***

When I speak of writing a History of Projects, I do not mean either of the introduction of, or continuing, necessary inventions, or the improvement of arts and sciences before known, but a short account of projects and projecting, as the word is allowed in the general acceptation at this present time; and I need not go far back for the original of the practice.

Invention of arts, with engines and handicraft instruments for their improvement, requires a chronology as far back as the eldest son of Adam, and has to this day afforded some new discovery in every age.

The building of the Ark by Noah, so far as you will allow it a human work, was the first project I read of; and, no question, seemed so ridiculous to the graver heads of that wise, though wicked, age that poor Noah was sufficiently bantered for it: and, had he not been set on work by a very peculiar direction from heaven, the good old man would certainly have been laughed out of it as a most senseless ridiculous project.

The building of Babel was a right project; for indeed the true definition of a project, according to modern acceptation, is, as is said before, a vast undertaking, too big to be managed, and therefore likely enough to come to nothing. And yet, as great as they are, it is certainly true of them all, even as the projectors propose: that, according to the old tale, if so many eggs are hatched, there will be so many chickens, and those chickens may lay so many eggs more, and those eggs produce so many chickens more, and so on. Thus it was most certainly true that if the people of the Old World could have built a house up to heaven, they should never be drowned again on earth, and they only had forgot to measure the height; that is, as in other projects, it only miscarried, or else it would have succeeded.

And yet, when all is done, that very building, and the incredible height it was carried, is a demonstration of the vast knowledge of that infant age of the world, who had no advantage of the experiments or invention of any before themselves.

> "Thus when our fathers, touched with guilt,
> That huge stupendous staircase built;
> We mock, indeed, the fruitless enterprise
> (For fruitless actions seldom pass for wise),
> But were the mighty ruins left, they'd show
> To what degree that untaught age did know."

I believe a very diverting account might be given of this, but I shall not attempt it. Some are apt to say with Solomon, "No new thing happens under the sun; but what is, has been:" yet I make no question but some considerable discovery has been made in these latter ages, and inventions of human origin produced, which the world was ever without before, either in whole or in part; and I refer only to two cardinal points, the use of the loadstone at sea, and the use of gunpowder and guns: both which, as to the inventing part, I believe the world owes as absolutely to those particular ages as it does the working in brass and iron to Tubal Cain, or the inventing of music to Jubal, his brother. As to engines and instruments for handicraftsmen, this age, I daresay, can show such as never were so much as thought of, much less imitated before; for I do not call that a real invention which has something before done like it I account that more properly an improvement. For handicraft instruments, I know none owes more to true genuine contrivance, without borrowing from any former use, than a mechanic engine contrived in our time called a knitting-frame, which, built with admirable symmetry, works really with a very happy success, and may be observed by the curious to have a more than ordinary composition; for which I refer to the engine itself, to be seen in every stocking-weaver's garret.

I shall trace the original of the projecting humour that now reigns no farther back than the year 1680, dating its birth as a monster then, though by times it had indeed something of life in the time of the late civil war. I allow, no age has been altogether without something of this nature, and some very happy projects are left to us as a taste of their success; as the water-houses for supplying of the city of London with water, and, since that, the New River – both very considerable undertakings, and perfect projects, adventured on the risk of success. In the reign of King

Charles I. infinite projects were set on foot for raising money without a Parliament: oppressing by monopolies and privy seals; but these are excluded our scheme as irregularities, for thus the French are as fruitful in projects as we; and these are rather stratagems than projects. After the Fire of London the contrivance of an engine to quench fires was a project the author was said to get well by, and we have found to be very useful. But about the year 1680 began the art and mystery of projecting to creep into the world. Prince Rupert, uncle to King Charles II., gave great encouragement to that part of it that respects engines and mechanical motions; and Bishop Wilkins added as much of the theory to it as writing a book could do. The prince has left us a metal called by his name; and the first project upon that was, as I remember, casting of guns of that metal and boring them – done both by a peculiar method of his own, and which died with him, to the great loss of the undertaker, who to that purpose had, with no small charge, erected a watermill at Hackney Marsh, known by the name of the Temple Mill, which mill very happily performed all parts of the work; and I have seen some of those guns on board the Royal Charles, a first-rate ship, being of a reddish colour, different either from brass or copper. I have heard some reasons of state assigned why that project was not permitted to go forward; but I omit them, because I have no good authority for them. After this we saw a floating-machine, to be wrought with horses, for the towing of great ships both against wind and tide; and another for the raising of ballast, which, as unperforming engines, had the honour of being made, exposed, tried, and laid by before the prince died.

If thus we introduce it into the world under the conduct of that prince, when he died it was left a hopeless brat, and had hardly any hand to own it, till the wreck-voyage before noted, performed so happily by Captain Phips, afterwards Sir William, whose strange performance set a great many heads on work to contrive something for themselves. He was immediately followed by my Lord Mordant, Sir John Narborough, and others from several parts, whose success made them soon weary of the work.

The project of the Penny Post, so well known and still practised, I cannot omit, nor the contriver, Mr. Dockwra, who has had the honour to have the injury done him in that affair repaired in some measure by the public justice of the Parliament. And, the experiment proving it to be a noble and useful design, the author must be remembered, wherever mention is made of that affair, to his very great reputation.

It was, no question, a great hardship for a man to be master of so fine a thought, that had both the essential ends of a project in it (public good and private want), and that the public should reap the benefit and the author be left out; the injustice of which, no doubt, discouraged many a good design. But since an alteration in public circumstances has recovered the lost attribute of justice, the like is not to be feared. And Mr. Dockwra has had the satisfaction to see the former injury disowned, and an honourable return made, even by them who did not the injury, in bare respect to his ingenuity.

A while before this several people, under the patronage of some great persons, had engaged in planting of foreign colonies (as William Penn, the Lord Shaftesbury, Dr. Cox, and others) in Pennsylvania, Carolina, East and West Jersey, and the like places, which I do not call projects, because it was only prosecuting what had been formerly begun. But here began the forming of public joint-stocks, which, together with the East India, African, and Hudson's Bay Companies, before established, begot a new trade, which we call by a new name stock-jobbing, which was at first only the simple occasional transferring of interest and shares from one to another, as persons alienated their estates; but by the industry of the Exchange brokers, who got the business into their hands, it became a trade, and one perhaps managed with the greatest intrigue, artifice, and trick that ever anything that appeared with a face of honesty could be handled with; for while the brokers held the box, they made the whole Exchange the gamesters, and raised and lowered the prices of stocks as they pleased, and always had both buyers and sellers who stood ready innocently to commit their money to the mercy of their mercenary tongues. This upstart of a trade, having tasted the sweetness of success which generally attends a novel proposal, introduces the illegitimate wandering object I speak of, as a proper engine to find work for the brokers. Thus stock-jobbing nursed projecting, and projecting, in return, has very diligently pimped for its foster-parent, till both are arrived to be public grievances, and indeed are now almost grown scandalous.

OF PROJECTORS.

***

Man is the worst of all God's creatures to shift for himself; no other animal is ever starved to death; nature without has provided them both food and clothes, and nature within has placed an instinct that never fails to direct them to proper means for a supply; but man must either work or starve, slave or die. He has indeed reason given him to direct him, and few who follow the dictates of that reason come to such unhappy exigences; but when by the errors of a man's youth he has reduced himself to such a degree of distress as to be absolutely without three things - money, friends, and health - he dies in a ditch, or in some worse place, a hospital.

Ten thousand ways there are to bring a man to this, and but very few to bring him out again.

Death is the universal deliverer, and therefore some who want courage to bear what they see before them, hang themselves for fear; for certainly self-destruction is the effect of cowardice in the highest extreme.

Others break the bounds of laws to satisfy that general law of nature, and turn open thieves, housebreakers, highwaymen, clippers, coiners, till they run the length of the gallows, and get a deliverance the nearest way at St. Tyburn.

Others, being masters of more cunning than their neighbours, turn their thoughts to private methods of trick and cheat, a modern way of thieving every jot as criminal, and in some degree worse than the other, by which honest men are gulled with fair pretences to part from their money, and then left to take their course with the author, who skulks behind the curtain of a protection, or in the Mint or Friars, and bids defiance as well to honesty as the law.

Others, yet urged by the same necessity, turn their thoughts to honest invention, founded upon the platform of ingenuity and integrity.

These two last sorts are those we call projectors; and as there was always more geese than swans, the number of the latter are very inconsiderable in comparison of the former; and as the greater number denominates the less, the just contempt we have of the former sort bespatters the other, who, like cuckolds, bear the reproach of other people's crimes.

A mere projector, then, is a contemptible thing, driven by his own desperate fortune to such a strait that he must be delivered by a miracle, or starve; and when he has beat his brains for some such miracle in vain, he finds no remedy but to paint up some bauble or other, as players make puppets talk big, to show like a strange thing, and then cry it up for a new invention, gets a patent for it, divides it into shares, and they must be sold. Ways and means are not wanting to swell the new whim to a vast magnitude; thousands and hundreds of thousands are the least of his discourse, and sometimes millions, till the ambition of some honest coxcomb is wheedled to part with his money for it, and then (nascitur ridiculus mus) the adventurer is left to carry on the project, and the projector laughs at him. The diver shall walk at the bottom of the Thames, the saltpetre maker shall build Tom T-d's pond into houses, the engineers build models and windmills to draw water, till funds are raised to carry it on by men who have more money than brains, and then Goodnight patent and invention; the projector has done his business and is gone.

But the honest projector is he who, having by fair and plain principles of sense, honesty, and ingenuity brought any contrivance to a suitable perfection, makes out what he pretends to, picks nobody's pocket, puts his project in execution, and contents himself with the real produce as the profit of his invention.

OF BANKS.

***

Banks, without question, if rightly managed are, or may be, of great advantage, especially to a trading people, as the English are; and, among many others, this is one particular case in which that benefit appears: that they bring down the interest of money, and take from the goldsmiths, scriveners, and others, who have command of running cash, their most delicious trade of making advantage of the necessities of the merchant in extravagant discounts and premiums for advance of money, when either large customs or foreign remittances call for disbursements beyond his common ability; for by the easiness of terms on which the merchant may have money, he is encouraged to venture further in trade than otherwise he would do. Not but that there are other great advantages a Royal Bank might procure in this kingdom, as has been seen in part by this; as advancing money to the Exchequer upon Parliamentary funds and securities, by which in time of a war our preparations for any expedition need not be in danger of miscarriage for want of money, though the taxes raised be not speedily paid, nor the Exchequer burthened with the excessive interests paid in former reigns upon anticipations of the revenue; landed men might be supplied with moneys upon securities on easier terms, which would prevent the loss of multitudes of estates, now ruined and devoured by insolent and merciless mortgagees, and the like. But now we unhappily see a Royal Bank established by Act of Parliament, and another with a large fund upon the Orphans' stock; and yet these advantages, or others, which we expected, not answered, though the pretensions in both have not been wanting at such time as they found it needful to introduce themselves into public esteem, by giving out prints of what they were rather able to do than really intended to practise. So that our having two banks at this time settled, and more erecting, has not yet been able to reduce the interest of money, not because the nature and foundation of their constitution does not tend towards it, but because, finding their hands full of better business, they are wiser than by being slaves to old obsolete proposals to lose the advantage of the great improvement they can make of their stock.

This, however, does not at all reflect on the nature of a bank, nor of the benefit it would be to the public trading part of the kingdom, whatever it may seem to do on the practice of the present. We find four or five banks now in view to be settled. I confess I expect no more from those to come than we have found from the past, and I think I make no broach on either my charity or good manners in saying so; and I reflect not upon any of the banks that are or shall be established for not doing what I mention, but for making such publications of what they would do. I cannot think any man had expected the Royal Bank should lend money on mortgages at 4 per cent. (nor was it much the better for them to make publication they would do so from the beginning of January next after their settlement), since to this day, as I am informed, they have not lent one farthing in that manner.

Our banks are indeed nothing but so many goldsmiths' shops, where the credit being high (and the directors as high) people lodge their money; and they – the directors, I mean – make their advantage of it. If you lay it at demand, they allow you nothing; if at time, 3 per cent.; and so would any goldsmith in Lombard Street have done before. But the very banks themselves are so awkward in lending, so strict, so tedious, so inquisitive, and withal so public in their taking securities, that men who are anything tender won't go to them; and so the easiness of borrowing money, so much designed, is defeated. For here is a private interest to be made, though it be a public one; and, in short, it is only a great trade carried on for the private gain of a few concerned in the original stock; and though we are to hope for great things, because they have promised them, yet they are all future that we know of.

And yet all this while a bank might be very beneficial to this kingdom; and this might be so, if either their own ingenuity or public authority would oblige them to take the public good into equal concern with their private interest.

To explain what I mean; banks, being established by public authority, ought also, as all public things are, to be under limitations and restrictions from that authority; and those limitations being regulated with a proper regard to the ease of trade in general, and the improvement of the stock in particular, would make a bank a useful, profitable thing indeed.

First, a bank ought to be of a magnitude proportioned to the trade of the country it is in, which this bank is so far from that it is no more to the whole than the least goldsmith's cash in Lombard Street is to the bank, from whence it comes to pass that already more banks are contriving. And I question not but banks in London will ere long be as frequent as lotteries; the consequence of which, in all probability, will be the diminishing their reputation, or a civil war with one another. It is true, the Bank of England has a capital stock; but yet, was that stock wholly clear of the public concern of the Government, it is not above a fifth part of what would be necessary to manage the whole business of the town – which it ought, though not to do, at least to be able to do. And I suppose I may venture to say above one-half of the stock of the present bank is taken up in the affairs of the Exchequer.

I suppose nobody will take this discourse for an invective against the Bank of England. I believe it is a very good fund, a very useful one, and a very profitable one. It has been useful to the Government, and it is profitable to the proprietors; and the establishing it at such a juncture, when our enemies were making great boasts of our poverty and want of money, was a particular glory to our nation, and the city in particular. That when the Paris Gazette informed the world that the Parliament had indeed given the king grants for raising money in funds to be paid in remote years, but money was so scarce that no anticipations could be procured; that just then, besides three millions paid into the Exchequer that spring on other taxes by way of advance, there was an overplus-stock to be found of 1,200,000 pounds sterling, or (to make it speak French) of above fifteen millions, which was all paid voluntarily into the Exchequer. Besides this, I believe the present Bank of England has been very useful to the Exchequer, and to supply the king with remittances for the payment of the army in Flanders, which has also, by the way, been very profitable to itself. But still this bank is not of that bulk that the business done here requires, nor is it able, with all the stock it has, to procure the great proposed benefit, the lowering the interest of money: whereas all foreign banks absolutely govern the interest, both at Amsterdam, Genoa, and other places. And this defect I conceive the multiplicity of banks cannot supply, unless a perfect understanding could be secured between them.

To remedy this defect, several methods might be proposed. Some I shall take the freedom to hint at:-

First, that the present bank increase their stock to at least five millions sterling, to be settled as they are already, with some small limitations to make the methods more beneficial.

Five millions sterling is an immense sum; to which add the credit of their cash, which would supply them with all the overplus-money in the town, and probably might amount to half as much more; and then the credit of running bills, which by circulating would, no question, be an equivalent to the other half: so that in stock, credit, and bank-bills the balance of their cash would be always ten millions sterling – a sum that everybody who can talk of does not understand.

But then to find business for all this stock, which, though it be a strange thing to think of, is nevertheless easy when it comes to be examined. And first for the business; this bank should enlarge the number of their directors, as they do of their stock, and should then establish several subcommittees, composed of their own members, who should have the directing of several offices relating to the distinct sorts of business they referred to, to be overruled and governed by the governor and directors in a body, but to have a conclusive power as to contracts. Of these there should be–

One office for loan of money for customs of goods, which by a plain method might be so ordered that the merchant might with ease pay the highest customs down, and so, by allowing the bank 4 per cent. advance, be first sure to secure the 10 pounds per cent. which the king allows for prompt payment at the Custom House, and be also freed from the troublesome work of finding bondsmen and securities for the money – which has exposed many a man to the tyranny of extents, either for himself or his friend, to his utter ruin, who under a more moderate prosecution had been able to pay all his debts, and by this method has been torn to pieces and disabled from making any tolerable proposal to his creditors. This is a scene of large business, and would, in proportion, employ a large cash, and it is the easiest thing in the world to make the bank the paymaster of all the large customs, and yet the merchant have so honourable a possession of his goods, as may be neither any diminution to his reputation or any hindrance to their sale.

As, for example, suppose I have 100 hogsheads of tobacco to import, whose customs by several duties come to 1,000 pounds, and want cash to clear them. I go with my bill of loading to the bank, who appoint their officer to enter the goods and pay the duties, which goods, so entered by the bank, shall give them title enough to any part, or the whole, without the trouble of bills of sale, or conveyances, defeasances, and the like. The goods are carried to a warehouse at the waterside, where the merchant has a free and public access to them, as if in his own warehouse and an honourable liberty to sell and deliver either the whole (paying their disburse) or a part without it, leaving but sufficient for the payment, and out of that part delivered, either by notes under the hand of the purchaser, or any other way, he may clear the same, without any exactions, but of 4 pounds per cent., and the rest are his own.

The ease this would bring to trade, the deliverance it would bring to the merchants from the insults of goldsmiths, and the honour it would give to our management of public imposts, with the advantages to the Custom House itself, and the utter destruction of extortion, would be such as would give a due value to the bank, and make all mankind acknowledge it to be a public good. The grievance of exactions upon merchants in this case is very great, and when I lay the blame on the goldsmiths, because they are the principal people made use of in such occasions, I include a great many other sorts of brokers and money-jobbing artists, who all get a snip out of the merchant. I myself have known a goldsmith in Lombard Street lend a man 700 pounds to pay the customs of a hundred pipes of Spanish wines; the wines were made over to him for security by bill of sale, and put into a cellar, of which the goldsmith kept the key; the merchant was to pay 6 pounds per cent. interest on the bond, and to allow 10 pounds percent. premium for advancing the money. When he had the wines in possession the owner could not send his cooper to look after them, but the goldsmith's man must attend all the while, for which he would be paid 5s. a day. If he brought a customer to see them, the goldsmith's man must show them. The money was lent for two months. He could not be admitted to sell or deliver a pipe of wine out single, or two or three at a time, as he might have sold them; but on a word or two spoken amiss to the goldsmith (or which he was pleased to take so), he would have none sold but the whole parcel together. By this usage the goods lay on hand, and every month the money remained the goldsmith demanded a guinea per cent. forbearance, besides the interest, till at last by leakage, decay, and other accidents, the wines began to lessen. Then the goldsmith begins to tell the merchant he is afraid the wines are not worth the money he has lent, and demands further security, and in a little while, growing higher and rougher, he tells him he must have his money. The merchant - too much at his mercy, because he cannot provide the money - is forced to consent to the sale; and the goods, being reduced to seventy pipes sound - wine and four unsound (the rest being sunk for filling up), were sold for 13 pounds per pipe the sound, and 3 pounds the unsound, which amounted to 922 pounds together.

	Pounds s. d
The cooper's bill came to	30 0 0
The cellarage a year and a half to	18 0 0
Interests on the bond to	63 0 0
The goldsmith's men for attendance	8 0 0
Allowance for advance of the money and forbearance	74 0 0
	======
	193 0 0

Principal money borrowed	700 0 0
	=======
	893 0 0
Due to the merchant	29 0 0
	=======
	922 0 0

By the moderatest computation that can be, these wines cost the merchant as follows:-

First Cost with Charges on Board.	Pounds s. d
In Lisbon 15 mille reis per pipe is 1,500 mille reis; exchange, at 6s. 4d. per mille rei	475 0 0
Freight to London, then at 3 pounds per ton	150 0 0
Assurance on 500 pounds at 2 per cent	10 0 0
Petty charges	5 0 0
	=======
	640 0 0

So that it is manifest by the extortion of this banker, the poor man lost the whole capital with freight and charges, and made but 29 pounds produce of a hundred pipes of wine.

One other office of this bank, and which would take up a considerable branch of the stock, is for lending money upon pledges, which should have annexed to it a warehouse and factory, where all sorts of goods might publicly be sold by the consent of the owners, to the great advantage of the owner, the bank receiving 4 pounds per cent. interest., and 2 per cent. commission for sale of the goods.

A third office should be appointed for discounting bills, tallies, and notes, by which all tallies of the Exchequer, and any part of the revenue, should at stated allowances be ready money to any person, to the great advantage of the Government, and ease of all such as are any ways concerned in public undertakings.

A fourth office for lending money upon land securities at 4 per cent. interest, by which the cruelty and injustice of mortgagees would be wholly restrained, and a register of mortgages might be very well kept, to prevent frauds.

A fifth office for exchanges and foreign correspondences.

A sixth for inland exchanges, where a very large field of business lies before them.

Under this head it will not be improper to consider that this method will most effectually answer all the notions and proposals of county banks; for by this office they would be all rendered useless and unprofitable, since one bank of the magnitude I mention, with a branch of its office set apart for that business, might with ease manage all the inland exchange of the kingdom.

By which such a correspondence with all the trading towns in England might be maintained, as that the whole kingdom should trade with the bank. Under the direction of this office a public cashier should be appointed in every county, to reside in the capital town as to trade (and in some counties more), through whose hands all the cash of the revenue of the gentry and of trade should be returned on the bank in London, and from the bank again on their cashier in every respective county or town, at the small exchange of 0.5 per cent., by which means all loss of money carried upon the road, to the encouragement of robbers and ruining of the country, who are sued for those robberies, would be more effectually prevented than by all the statutes against highwaymen that are or can be made.

As to public advancings of money to the Government, they may be left to the directors in a body, as all other disputes and contingent cases are; and whoever examines these heads of business apart, and has any judgment in the particulars, will, I suppose, allow that a stock of ten millions may find employment in them, though it be indeed a very great sum.

I could offer some very good reasons why this way of management by particular offices for every particular sort of business is not only the easiest, but the safest, way of executing an affair of such variety and consequence; also I could state a method for the proceedings of those private offices, their conjunction with and dependence on the general court of the directors, and how the various accounts should centre in one general capital account of stock, with regulations and appeals; but I believe them to be needless – at least, in this place.

If it be objected here that it is impossible for one joint-stock to go through the whole business of the kingdom, I answer, I believe it is not either impossible or impracticable, particularly on this one account: that almost all the country business would be managed by running bills, and those the longest abroad of any, their distance keeping them out, to the increasing the credit, and consequently the stock of the bank.

OF THE MULTIPLICITY OF BANKS.

***

What is touched at in the foregoing part of this chapter refers to one bank royal to preside, as it were, over the whole cash of the kingdom: but because some people do suppose this work fitter for many banks than for one, I must a little consider that head. And first, allowing those many banks could, without clashing, maintain a constant correspondence with one another, in passing each other's bills as current from one to another, I know not but it might be better performed by many than by one; for as harmony makes music in sound, so it produces success in business.

A civil war among merchants is always the rain of trade: I cannot think a multitude of banks could so consist with one another in England as to join interests and uphold one another's credit, without joining stocks too; I confess, if it could be done, the convenience to trade would be visible.

If I were to propose which way these banks should be established, I answer, allowing a due regard to some gentlemen who have had thoughts of the same (whose methods I shall not so much as touch upon, much less discover; my thoughts run upon quite different methods, both for the fund and the establishment).

Every principal town in England is a corporation, upon which the fund may be settled, which will sufficiently answer the difficult and chargeable work of suing for a corporation by patent or Act of Parliament.

A general subscription of stock being made, and by deeds of settlement placed in the mayor and aldermen of the city or corporation for the time being, in trust, to be declared by deeds of uses, some of the directors being always made members of the said corporation, and joined in the trust; the bank hereby becomes the public stock of the town (something like what they call the rentes of the townhouse in France), and is managed in the name of the said corporation, to whom the directors are accountable, and they back again to the general court.

For example: suppose the gentlemen or tradesmen of the county of Norfolk, by a subscription of cash, design to establish a bank. The subscriptions being made, the stock is paid into the chamber of the city of Norwich, and managed by a court of directors, as all banks are, and chosen out of the subscribers, the mayor only of the city to be always one; to be managed in the name of the corporation of the city of Norwich, but for the uses in a deed of trust to be made by the subscribers, and mayor and aldermen, at large mentioned. I make no question but a bank thus settled would have as firm a foundation as any bank need to have, and every way answer the ends of a corporation.

Of these sorts of banks England might very well establish fifteen, at the several towns hereafter mentioned. Some of which, though they are not the capital towns of the counties, yet are more the centre of trade, which in England runs in veins, like mines of metal in the earth:

Canterbury. Salisbury. Exeter. Bristol. Worcester. Shrewsbury. Manchester. Newcastle-upon-Tyne. Leeds, or Halifax, or York. Warwick or Birmingham. Oxford or Reading. Bedford. Norwich. Colchester.

Every one of these banks to have a cashier in London, unless they could all have a general correspondence and credit with the bank royal.

These banks in their respective counties should be a general staple and factory for the manufactures of the said county, where every man that had goods made, might have money at a small interest for advance, the goods in the meantime being sent forward to market, to a warehouse for that purpose erected in London, where they should be disposed of to all the advantages the owner could expect, paying only 1 per cent. commission. Or if the maker wanted credit in London either for Spanish wool, cotton, oil, or any goods, while his goods were in the warehouse of the said bank, his bill should be paid by the bank to the full value of his goods, or at least within a small matter. These banks, either by correspondence with each other, or an order to their cashier in London, might with ease so pass each other's bills that a man who has cash at Plymouth, and wants money at Berwick, may transfer his cash at Plymouth to Newcastle in half-an-hour's time, without either hazard, or charge, or time, allowing only 0.5 per cent. exchange; and so of all the most distant parts of the kingdom. Or if he wants money at Newcastle, and has goods at Worcester or at any other clothing town, sending his goods to be sold by the factory of the bank of Worcester, he may remit by the bank to Newcastle, or anywhere else, as readily as if his goods were sold and paid for and no exactions made upon him for the convenience he enjoys.

This discourse of banks, the reader is to understand, to have no relation to the present posture of affairs, with respect to the scarcity of current money, which seems to have put a stop to that part of a stock we call credit, which always is, and indeed must be, the most essential part of a bank, and without which no bank can pretend to subsist – at least, to advantage.

A bank is only a great stock of money put together, to be employed by some of the subscribers, in the name of the rest, for the benefit of the whole. This stock of money subsists not barely on the profits of its own stock (for that would be inconsiderable), but upon the contingencies and accidents which multiplicity of business occasions. As, for instance, a man that comes for money, and knows he may have it tomorrow; perhaps he is in haste, and won't take it today: only, that he may be sure of it tomorrow, he takes a memorandum under the hand of the officer, that he shall have it whenever he calls for it, and this memorandum we call a bill. tomorrow, when he intended to fetch his money, comes a man to him for money, and, to save himself the labour of telling, he gives him the memorandum or bill aforesaid for his money; this second man does as the first, and a third does as he did, and so the bill runs about a mouth, two or three. And this is that we call credit, for by the circulation of a quantity of these bills, the bank enjoys the full benefit of as much stock in real value as the suppositious value of the bills amounts to; and wherever this credit fails, this advantage fails; for immediately all men come for their money, and the bank must die of itself: for I am sure no bank, by the simple improvement of their single stock, can ever make any considerable advantage.

I confess, a bank who can lay a fund for the security of their bills, which shall produce first an annual profit to the owner, and yet make good the passant bill, may stand, and be advantageous, too, because there is a real and a suppositious value both, and the real always ready to make good the suppositious: and this I know no way to bring to pass but by land, which, at the same time that it lies transferred to secure the value of every bill given out, brings in a separate profit to the owner; and this way no question but the whole kingdom might be a bank to itself, though no ready money were to be found in it.

I had gone on in some sheets with my notion of land being the best bottom for public banks, and the easiness of bringing it to answer all the ends of money deposited with double advantage, but I find myself happily prevented by a gentleman who has published the very same, though since this was wrote; and I was always master of so much wit as to hold my tongue while they spoke who understood the thing better than myself.

Mr. John Asgill, of Lincoln's Inn, in a small tract entitled, "Several Assertions proved, in order to create another Species of Money than Gold and Silver," has so distinctly handled this very case, with such strength of argument, such clearness of reason, such a judgment, and such a style, as all the ingenious part of the world must acknowledge themselves extremely obliged to him for that piece.

At the sight of which book I laid by all that had been written by me on that subject, for I had much rather confess myself incapable of handling that point like him, than have convinced the world of it by my impertinence.

OF THE HIGHWAYS.

***

It is a prodigious charge the whole nation groans under for the repair of highways, which, after all, lie in a very ill posture too. I make no question but if it was taken into consideration by those who have the power to direct it, the kingdom might be wholly eased of that burden, and the highways be kept in good condition, which now lie in a most shameful manner in most parts of the kingdom, and in many places wholly unpassable, from whence arise tolls and impositions upon passengers and travellers, and, on the other hand, trespasses and encroachments upon lands adjacent, to the great damage of the owners.

The rate for the highways is the most arbitrary and unequal tax in the kingdom: in some places two or three rates of sixpence per pound in the year; in others the whole parish cannot raise wherewith to defray the charge, either by the very bad condition of the road or distance of materials; in others the surveyors raise what they never expend; and the abuses, exactions, connivances, frauds, and embezzlements are innumerable.

The Romans, while they governed this island, made it one of their principal cares to make and repair the highways of the kingdom, and the chief roads we now use are of their marking out; the consequence of maintaining them was such, or at least so esteemed, that they thought it not below them to employ their legionary troops in the work; and it was sometimes the business of whole armies, either when in winter quarters or in the intervals of truce or peace with the natives. Nor have the Romans left us any greater tokens of their grandeur and magnificence than the ruins of those causeways and street-ways which are at this day to be seen in many parts of the kingdom, some of which have by the visible remains been discovered to traverse the whole kingdom, and others for more than a hundred miles are to be traced from colony to colony, as they had particular occasion. The famous highway or street called Watling Street, which some will tell you began at London Stone, and passing that very street in the City which we to this day call by that name, went on west to that spot where Tyburn now stands, and then turned northwest in so straight a line to St. Albans that it is now the exactest road (in one line for twenty miles) in the kingdom; and though disused now as the chief, yet is as good, and, I believe, the best road to St. Albans, and is still called the Streetway. From whence it is traced into Shropshire, above a hundred and sixty miles, with a multitude of visible antiquities upon it, discovered and described very accurately by Mr. Cambden. The Fosse, another Roman work, lies at this day as visible, and as plain a high causeway, of above thirty feet broad, ditched on either side, and coped and paved where need is – as exact and every jot as beautiful as the king's new road through Hyde Park, in which figure it now lies from near Marshfield to Cirencester, and again from Cirencester to the Hill, three miles on this side Gloucester, which is not less than twenty-six miles, and is made use of as the great road to those towns, and probably has been so for a thousand years with little repairs.

If we set aside the barbarity and customs of the Romans as heathens, and take them as a civil government, we must allow they were the pattern of the whole world for improvement and increase of arts and learning, civilising and methodising nations and countries conquered by their valour; and if this was one of their great cares, that consideration ought to move something. But to the great example of that generous people I will add three arguments:–

1. It is useful, and that as it is convenient for carriages, which in a trading country is a great help to negotiation, and promotes universal correspondence, without which our inland trade could not be managed. And under this head I could name a thousand conveniences of a safe, pleasant, well-repaired highway, both to the inhabitant and the traveller, but I think it is needless.

2. It is easy. I question not to make it appear it is easy to put all the highroads, especially in England, in a noble figure; large, dry, and clean; well drained, and free from floods, unpassable sloughs, deep cart-ruts, high ridges, and all the inconveniences they now are full of; and, when once done, much easier still to be maintained so.

3. It may be cheaper, and the whole assessment for the repairs of highways for ever be dropped or applied to other uses for the public benefit.

Here I beg the reader's favour for a small digression.

I am not proposing this as an undertaker, or setting a price to the public for which I will perform it, like one of the projectors I speak of, but laying open a project for the performance, which, whenever the public affairs will admit our governors to consider of, will be found so feasible that no question they may find undertakers enough for the performance; and in this undertaking age I do not doubt but it would be easy at any time to procure persons at their own charge to perform it for any single county, as a pattern and experiment for the whole kingdom.

The proposal is as follows:- First, that an Act of Parliament be made with liberty for the undertakers to dig and trench, to cut down hedges and trees, or whatever is needful for ditching, draining and carrying off water, cleaning, enlarging and levelling the roads, with power to lay open or enclose lands; to encroach into lands; dig, raise, and level fences; plant and pull up hedges or trees (for the enlarging, widening, and draining the highways), with power to turn either the roads or watercourses, rivers and brooks, as by the directors of the works shall be found needful, always allowing satisfaction to be first made to the owners of such lands (either by assigning to them equivalent lands or payment in money, the value to be adjusted by two indifferent persons to be named by the Lord Chancellor or Lord Keeper for the time being), and no watercourse to be turned from any watermill without satisfaction first made both to the landlord and tenant.

But before I proceed, I must say a word or two to this article.

The chief, and almost the only, cause of the deepness and foulness of the roads is occasioned by the standing water, which (for want of due care to draw it off by scouring and opening ditches and drains, and other watercourses, and clearing of passages) soaks into the earth, and softens it to such a degree that it cannot bear the weight of horses and carriages; to prevent which, the power to dig, trench, and cut down, mentioned above will be of absolute necessity. But because the liberty seems very large, and some may think it is too great a power to be granted to any body of men over their neighbours, it is answered:–

1. It is absolutely necessary, or the work cannot be done, and the doing of the work is of much greater benefit than the damage can amount to.

2. Satisfaction to be made to the owner (and that first, too, before the damage be done) is an unquestionable equivalent; and both together, I think, are a very full answer to any objection in that case.

Besides this Act of Parliament, a commission must be granted to fifteen at least, in the name of the undertakers, to whom every county shall have power to join ten, who are to sit with the said fifteen so often and so long as the said fifteen do sit for affairs relating to that county, which fifteen, or any seven of them, shall be directors of the works, to be advised by the said ten, or any five of them, in matters of right and claim, and the said ten to adjust differences in the countries, and to have right by process to appeal in the name either of lords of manors, or privileges of towns or corporations, who shall be either damaged or encroached upon by the said work. All appeals to be heard and determined immediately by the said Lord Chancellor, or commission from him, that the work may receive no interruption.

This commission shall give power to the said fifteen to press waggons, carts, and horses, oxen and men, and detain them to work a certain limited time, and within certain limited space of miles from their own dwellings, and at a certain rate of payment. No men, horses, or carts to be pressed against their consent during the times of hay-time or harvest, or upon market-days, if the person aggrieved will make affidavit he is obliged to be with his horses or carts at the said markets.

It is well known to all who have any knowledge of the condition the highways in England now lie in that in most places there is a convenient distance land left open for travelling, either for driving of cattle, or marching of troops of horse, with perhaps as few lanes or defiles as in any countries. The crossroads, which are generally narrow, are yet broad enough in most places for two carriages to pass; but, on the other hand, we have on most of the highroads a great deal, if waste land thrown in (as it were, for an overplus to the highway), which, though it be used of course by cattle and travellers on occasion, is indeed no benefit at all either to the traveller as a road or to the poor as a common, or to the lord of the manor as a waste; upon it grows neither timber nor grass, in any quantity answerable to the land, but, though to no purpose, is trodden down, poached, and overrun by drifts of cattle in the winter, or spoiled with the dust in the summer. And this I have observed in many parts of England to be as good land as any of the neighbouring enclosures, as capable of improvement, and to as good purpose.

These lands only being enclosed and manured, leaving the roads to dimensions without measure sufficient, are the fund upon which I build the prodigious stock of money that must do this work. These lands (which I shall afterwards make an essay to value), being enclosed, will be either saleable to raise money, or fit to exchange with those gentlemen who must part with some land where the ways are narrow, always reserving a quantity of these lands to be let out to tenants, the rent to be paid into the public stock or bank of the undertakers, and to be reserved for keeping the ways in the same repair, and the said bank to forfeit the lands if they are not so maintained.

Another branch of the stock must be hands (for a stock of men is a stock of money), to which purpose every county, city, town, and parish shall be rated at a set price, equivalent to eight years' payment, for the repair of highways, which each county, shall raise, not by assessment in money, but by pressing of men, horses, and carriages for the work (the men, horses, to be employed by the directors); in which case all corporal punishments - as of whippings, stocks, pillories, houses of correction, be easily transmitted to a certain number of days' work on the highways, and in consideration of this provision of men the country should for ever after be acquitted of any contribution, either in money or work, for repair of the highways - building of bridges excepted.

There lie some popular objections against this undertaking; and the first is (the great controverted point of England) enclosure of the common, which tends to depopulation, and injures the poor.

2. Who shall be judges or surveyors of the work, to oblige the undertakers to perform to a certain limited degree?

For the first, "the enclosure of the common" - a clause that runs as far as to an encroachment upon Magna Charta, and a most considerable branch of the property of the poor - I answer it thus:-

1. The lands we enclose are not such as from which the poor do indeed reap any benefit - or, at least, any that is considerable.

2. The bank and public stock, who are to manage this great undertaking, will have so many little labours to perform and offices to bestow, that are fit only for labouring poor persons to do, as will put them in a condition to provide for the poor who are so injured, that can work; and to those who cannot, may allow pensions for overseeing, supervising, and the like, which will be more than equivalent.

3. For depopulations, the contrary should be secured, by obliging the undertakers, at such and such certain distances, to erect cottages, two at least in a place (which would be useful to the work and safety of the traveller), to which should be an allotment of land, always sufficient to invite the poor inhabitant, in which the poor should be tenant for life gratis, doing duty upon the highway as should be appointed, by which, and many other methods, the poor should be great gainers by the proposal, instead of being injured.

4. By this erecting of cottages at proper distances a man might travel over all England as through a street, where he could never want either rescue from thieves or directions for his way.

5. This very undertaking, once duly settled, might in a few years so order it that there should be no poor for the common; and, if so, what need of a common for the poor? Of which in its proper place.

As to the second objection, "Who should oblige the undertakers to the performance?" I answer–

1. Their Commission and charter should become void, and all their stock forfeit, and the lands enclosed and unsold remain as a pledge, which would be security sufficient.

2. The ten persons chosen out of every county should have power to inspect and complain, and the Lord Chancellor, upon such complaint, to make a survey, and to determine by a jury, in which case, on default, they shall be obliged to proceed.

3. The lands settled on the bank shall be liable to be extended for the uses mentioned, if the same at any time be not maintained in the condition at first provided, and the bank to be amerced upon complaint of the country.

These and other conditions, which on a legal settlement to be made by wiser heads than mine might be thought on, I do believe would form a constitution so firm, so fair, and so equally advantageous to the country, to the poor, and to the public, as has not been put in practice in these later ages of the world. To discourse of this a little in general, and to instance in a place perhaps that has not its fellow in the kingdom - the parish of Islington, in Middlesex. There lies through this large parish the greatest road in England, and the most frequented, especially by cattle for Smithfield market; this great road has so many branches, and lies for so long a way through the parish, and withal has the inconvenience of a clayey ground, and no gravel at hand, that, modestly speaking, the parish is not able to keep it in repair; by which means several crossroads in the parish lie wholly unpassable, and carts and horses (and men too) have been almost buried in holes and sloughs; and the main road itself has for many years lain in a very ordinary condition, which occasioned several motions in Parliament to raise a toll at Highgate for the performance of what it was impossible the parish should do, and yet was of so absolute necessity to be done. And is it not very probable the parish of Islington would part with all the waste land upon their roads, to be eased of the intolerable assessment for repair of the highway, and answer the poor, who reap but a small benefit from it, some other way? And yet I am free to affirm that for a grant of waste and almost useless land, lying open to the highway (those lands to be improved, as they might easily be), together with the eight years' assessment to be provided in workmen, a noble, magnificent causeway might be erected, with ditches on either side, deep enough to receive the water, and drains sufficient to carry it off, which causeway should be four feet high at least, and from thirty to forty feet broad, to reach from London to Barnet, paved in the middle, to keep it coped, and so supplied with gravel and other proper materials as should secure it from decay with small repairing.

I hope no man would be so weak now as to imagine that by lands lying open to the road, to be assigned to the undertakers, I should mean that all

Finchley Common should be enclosed and sold for this work; but, lest somebody should start such a preposterous objection, I think it is not improper to mention, that wherever a highway is to be carried over a large common, forest, or waste, without a hedge on either hand for a certain distance, there the several parishes shall allot the directors a certain quantity of the common, to lie parallel with the road, at a proportioned number of feet to the length and breadth of the said road – consideration also to be had to the nature of the ground; or else, giving them only room for the road directly shall suffer them to inclose in any one spot so much of the said common as shall be equivalent to the like quantity of land lying by the road. Thus where the land is good and the materials for erecting a causeway near, the less land may serve; and on the contrary, the more; but in general allowing them the quantity of land proportioned to the length of the causeway, and forty rods in breadth: though where the land is poor, as on downs and plains, the proportion must be considered to be adjusted by the country.

Another point for the dimensions of roads should be adjusted; and the breadth of them, I think, cannot be less than thus:

From London every way ten miles the high post-road to be built full forty feet in breadth and four feet high, the ditches eight feet broad and six feet deep, and from thence onward thirty feet, and so in proportion. crossroads to be twenty feet broad, and ditches proportioned; no lanes and passes less than nine feet without ditches.

The middle of the high causeways to be paved with stone, chalk, or gravel, and kept always two feet higher than the sides, that the water might have a free course into the ditches; and persons kept in constant employ to fill up holes, let out water, open drains, and the like, as there should be occasion – a proper work for highwaymen and such malefactors, as might on those services be exempted from the gallows.

It may here be objected that eight years' assessment to be demanded down is too much in reason to expect any of the poorer sort can pay; as, for instance, if a farmer who keeps a team of horse be at the common assessment to work a week, it must not be put so hard upon any man as to work eight weeks together. It is easy to answer this objection.

So many as are wanted, must be had; if a farmer's team cannot be spared without prejudice to him so long together, he may spare it at sundry times, or agree to be assessed, and pay the assessment at sundry payments; and the bank may make it as easy to them as they please.

Another method, however, might be found to fix this work at once. As suppose a bank be settled for the highways of the county of Middlesex, which as they are, without doubt, the most used of any in the kingdom, so also they require the more charge, and in some parts lie in the worst condition of any in the kingdom.

If the Parliament fix the charge of the survey of the highways upon a bank to be appointed for that purpose for a certain term of years, the bank undertaking to do the work, or to forfeit the said settlement.

As thus: suppose the tax on land and tenements for the whole county of Middlesex does, or should be so ordered as it might, amount to 20,000 pounds per annum more or less, which it now does, and much more, including the work of the farmers' teams, which must be accounted as money, and is equivalent to it, with some allowance to be rated for the city of London, who do enjoy the benefit, and make the most use of the said roads, both for carrying of goods and bringing provisions to the city, and therefore in reason ought to contribute towards the highways (for it is a most unequal thing that the road from Highgate to Smithfield Market, by which the whole city is, in a manner, supplied with live cattle, and the road by those cattle horribly spoiled, should lie all upon that one parish of Islington to repair); wherefore I will suppose a rate for the highways to be gathered through the city of London of 10,000 pounds per annum more, which may be appointed to be paid by carriers, drovers, and all such as keep teams, horses, or coaches, and the like, or many ways, as is most equal and reasonable; the waste lands in the said county, which by the consent of the parishes, lords of the manors, and proprietors shall be allowed to the undertakers, when inclosed and let out, may (the land in Middlesex generally letting high) amount to 5,000 pounds per annum more. If, then, an Act of Parliament be procured to settle the tax of 30,000 pounds per annum for eight years, most of which will be levied in workmen and not in money, and the waste lands for ever, I dare be bold to offer that the highways for the whole county of Middlesex should be put into the following form, and the 5,000 pounds per annum land be bound to remain as a security to maintain them so, and the county be never burdened with any further tax for the repair of the highways.

And that I may not propose a matter in general, like begging the question, without demonstration, I shall enter into the particulars how it may be performed, and that under these following heads of articles:

1. What the charge will be.
2. How to be raised.
3. What security for performance.
4. What profit to the undertaker.

1. WHAT I PROPOSE TO DO TO THE HIGHWAYS. – I answer first, not repair them; and yet secondly, not alter them – that is, not alter the course they run; but perfectly build them as a fabric. And, to descend to the particulars, it is first necessary to note which are the roads I mean, and their dimensions.

First, the high post-roads, and they are for the county of Middlesex as follows:

From London to	Miles.
Staines, which is	15
Colebrook is from Hounslow	5
Uxbridge	15
Bushey, the Old Street-way	10
Barnet, or near it	9
Waltham Cross, in Ware Road	11
Bow	2
	==
	67

Besides these, there, are crossroads, bye-roads, and lanes, which must also be looked after; and that some of them may be put into condition, others may be wholly slighted and shut up, or made drift-ways, bridleways, or footways, as may be thought convenient by the counties.

The crossroads of most repute are as follows:

From		Miles.
London	Hackney, Old Ford, and Bow	5
Hackney	Dalston and Islington	2
Ditto	Hornsey, Muswell Hill, to Whetstone	8
Tottenham	The Chase, Southgate, &c. called Green Lanes	6
Enfield Wash	Enfield Town, Whetstone, Totteridge, to Edgworth	10

London	Hampstead, Hendon, and Edgworth	8
Edgworth	Stanmore, to Pinner, to Uxbridge	8
London	Harrow and Pinner Green	11
Ditto	Chelsea, Fulham	4
Brentford	Thistleworth, Twittenham, and Kingston	6
Kingston	Staines, Colebrook, and Uxbridge	17
Ditto	Chertsey Bridge	5
		===
		90
Overplus miles		50
		===
		140

And because there may be many parts of the crossroads which cannot be accounted in the number abovementioned, or may slip my knowledge or memory, I allow an overplus of 50 miles, to be added to the 90 miles above, which together make the crossroads of Middlesex to be 140 miles.

For the bye-lanes such as may be slighted need nothing but to be ditched up; such as are for private use of lands, for carrying off corn, and driving cattle, are to be looked after by private hands.

But of the last sort, not to be accounted by particulars, in the small county of Middlesex we cannot allow less in cross-bye-lanes, from village to village, and from dwelling-houses which stand out of the way to the roads, than 1,000 miles.

So in the whole county I reckon up–

	Miles.
Of the high post-road	67
Of cross-roads less public	140
Of bye-lanes and passes	1,000
	=====
	1,207

These are the roads I mean, and thus divided under their several denominations.

To the question, what I would do to them I answer–

(1). For the sixty-seven miles of high post-road I propose to throw up a firm strong causeway well-bottomed, six feet high in the middle and four feet on the side, faced with brick or stone, and crowned with gravel, chalk, or stone, as the several counties they are made through will afford, being forty-four feet in breadth, with ditches on either side eight feet broad and four feet deep; so the whole breadth will be sixty feet, if the ground will permit.

At the end of every two miles, or such like convenient distances, shall be a cottage erected, with half an acre of ground allowed, which shall be given gratis, with one shilling per week wages, to such poor man of the parish as shall be approved, who shall, once at least every day, view his walk, to open passages for the water to run into the ditches, to fill up holes or soft places.

Two riders shall be allowed to be always moving the rounds, to view everything out of repair, and make report to the directors, and to see that the cottagers do their duty.

(2). For the 140 miles of crossroad a like causeway to be made, but of different dimensions – the breadth twenty feet, if the ground will allow it; the ditches four feet broad, three feet deep; the height in the middle three feet, and on the sides one foot, or two where it may be needful; to be also crowned with gravel, and one shilling per week to be allowed to the poor of every parish, the constables to be bound to find a man to walk on the highway every division for the same purpose as the cottagers do on the greater roads.

Posts to be set up at every turning to note whither it goes, for the direction of strangers, and how many miles distant.

(3). For the 1,000 miles of bye-lanes, only good and sufficient care to keep them in repair as they are, and to carry the water off by clearing and cutting the ditches, and laying materials where they are wanted.

This is what I propose to do to them, and what, if once performed, I suppose all people would own to be an undertaking both useful and honourable.

2. The second question I propose to give an account of is, WHAT THE CHARGE WILL BE, which I account thus.

The work of the great causeway I propose, shall not cost less than ten shillings per foot (supposing materials to be bought, carriage, and men's labour to be all hired), which for sixty-seven miles in length is no less than the sum of 176,880 pounds; as thus:

Every mile accounted at 1,760 yards, and three feet to the yard, is 5,280 feet, which at ten shillings per foot is 2,640 pounds per mile, and that, again, multiplied by sixty-seven, makes the sum of 176,880 pounds, into which I include the charge of watercourses, mills to throw off water where needful, drains,

To this charge must be added, ditching to inclose land for thirty cottages, and building thirty cottages at 40 pounds each, which is 1,200 pounds.

The work of the smaller causeway I propose to finish at the rate of a shilling per foot, which being for 149 miles in length, at 5,280 feet per mile, amounts to 36,960 pounds.

Ditching, draining, and repairing 1,000 miles, Supposed at three shillings per rod, as for 320,000 rods, is 48,000 pounds, which, added to the two former accounts, is thus:

	Pounds
The high post-roads, or the great causeway	178,080
The small causeway	36,960
Bye-lanes, &c.	48,000
	========
	263,040

If I were to propose some measures for the easing this charge, I could perhaps lay a scheme down how it may be performed for less than one-half of this charge.

As first, by a grant of the court at the Old Bailey whereby all such criminals as are condemned to die for smaller crimes may, instead of transportation, be ordered a year's work on the highways; others, instead of whippings, a proportioned time, and the like; which would, by a moderate computation, provide us generally a supply of 200 workmen, and coming in as fast as they go off; and let the overseers alone to make them work.

Secondly, by an agreement with the Guinea Company to furnish 200 negroes, who are generally persons that do a great deal of work; and all these are subsisted very reasonably out of a public storehouse.

Thirdly, by carts and horses to be bought, not hired, with a few able carters; and to the other a few workmen that have judgment to direct the rest, and thus I question not the great causeway shall be done for four shillings per foot charge; but of this by-the-bye.

Fourthly, a liberty to ask charities and benevolences to the work.

3. To the question, HOW THIS MONEY SHALL BE RAISED. I think if the Parliament settle the tax on the county for eight years at 30,000 pounds per annum, no man need ask how it shall be raised . . . It will be easy enough to raise the money; and no parish can grudge to pay a little larger rate for such a term, on condition never to be taxed for the highways any more.

Eight years' assessment at 30,000 pounds per annum is enough to afford to borrow the money by way of anticipation, if need be; the fund being secured by Parliament, and appropriated to that use and no other.

4. As to WHAT SECURITY FOR PERFORMANCE.

The lands which are inclosed may be appropriated by the same Act of Parliament to the bank and undertakers, upon condition of performance, and to be forfeit to the use of the several parishes to which they belong, in case upon presentation by the grand juries, and reasonable time given, any part of the roads in such and such parishes be not kept and maintained in that posture they are proposed to be. Now the lands thus settled are an eternal security to the country for the keeping the roads in repair; because, they will always be of so much value over the needful charge as will make it worth while to the undertakers to preserve their title to them; and the tenure of them being so precarious as to be liable to forfeiture on default, they will always be careful to uphold the causeways.

Lastly, WHAT PROFIT TO THE UNDERTAKERS. For we must allow them to gain, and that considerably, or no man would undertake such a work.

To this I propose: first, during the work, allow them out of the stock 3,000 pounds per annum for management.

After the work is finished, so much of the 5,000 pounds per annum as can be saved, and the roads kept in good repair, let be their own; and if the lands secured be not of the value of 5,000 pounds a year, let so much of the eight years' tax be set apart as may purchase land to make them up; if they come to more, let the benefit be to the adventurers.

It may be objected here that a tax of 30,000 pounds for eight years will come in as fast as it can well be laid out, and so no anticipations will be requisite; for the whole work proposed cannot be probably finished in less time; and, if so,

	Pounds
The charge of the county amounts to	240,000
The lands saved eight years' revenue	40,000
	========

280,000

To this I say I would have the undertakers bound to accept the salary of 3,000 pounds per annum for management, and if a whole year's tax can be spared, either leave it unraised upon the country, or put it in bank to be improved against any occasion – of building, perhaps, a great bridge; or some very wet season or frost may so damnify the works as to make them require more than ordinary repair. But the undertakers should make no private advantage of such an overplus; there might be ways enough found for it.

Another objection lies against the possibility of inclosing the lands upon the waste, which generally belongs to some manor, whose different tenures may be so cross, and so otherwise encumbered, that even the lords of those manors, though they were willing, could not convey them.

This may be answered in general, that an Act of Parliament is omnipotent with respect to titles and tenures of land, and can empower lords and tenants to consent to what else they could not; as to particulars, they cannot be answered till they are proposed; but there is no doubt but an Act of Parliament may adjust it all in one head.

What a kingdom would England be if this were performed in all the counties of it! And yet I believe it is feasible, even in the worst. I have narrowly deserved all the considerable ways in that unpassable county of Sussex, which (especially in some parts in the wild, as they very properly call it, of the county) hardly admits the country people to travel to markets in winter, and makes corn dear at market because it cannot be brought, and cheap at the farmer's house because he cannot carry it to market; yet even in that county would I undertake to carry on this proposal, and that to great advantage, if backed with the authority of an Act of Parliament.

I have seen in that horrible country the road, sixty to a hundred yards broad, lie from side to side all poached with cattle, the land of no manner of benefit, and yet no going with a horse, but at every step up to the shoulders, full of sloughs and holes, and covered with standing water. It costs them incredible sums of money to repair them; and the very places that are mended would fright a young traveller to go over them. The Romans mastered this work, and by a firm causeway made a highway quite through this deep country, through Darkin in Surrey to Stansted, and thence to Okeley, and so on to Arundel; its name tells us what it was made of (for it was called Stone Street), and many visible parts of it remain to this day.

Now would any lord of a manor refuse to allow forty yards in breadth out of that road I mentioned, to have the other twenty made into a firm, fair, and pleasant causeway over that wilderness of a country?

Or would not any man acknowledge that putting this country into a condition for carriages and travellers to pass would be a great work? The gentlemen would find the benefit of it in the rent of their land and price of their timber; the country people would find the difference in the sale of their goods, which now they cannot carry beyond the first market town, and hardly thither; and the whole county would reap an advantage a hundred to one greater than the charge of it. And since the want we feel of any convenience is generally the first motive to contrivance for a remedy, I wonder no man over thought of some expedient for so considerable a defect.

OF ASSURANCES.

***

Assurances among merchants, I believe, may plead prescription, and have been of use time out of mind in trade, though perhaps never so much a trade as now.

It is a compact among merchants. Its beginning being an accident to trade, and arose from the disease of men's tempers, who, having run larger adventures in a single bottom than afterwards they found convenient, grew fearful and uneasy; and discovering their uneasiness to others, who perhaps had no effects in the same vessel, they offer to bear part of the hazard for part of the profit: convenience made this a custom, and custom brought it into a method, till at last it becomes a trade.

I cannot question the lawfulness of it, since all risk in trade is for gain, and when I am necessitated to have a greater cargo of goods in such or such a bottom than my stock can afford to lose, another may surely offer to go a part with me; and as it is just if I give another part of the gain, he should run part of the risk, so it is as just that if he runs part of my risk, he should have part of the gain. Some object the disparity of the premium to the hazard, when the insurer runs the risk of 100 pounds on the seas from Jamaica to London for 40s., which, say they, is preposterous and unequal. Though this objection is hardly worth answering to men of business, yet it looks something fair to them that know no better; and for the information of such, I trouble the reader with a few heads:

First, they must consider the insurer is out no stock.

Secondly, it is but one risk the insurer runs; whereas the assured has had a risk out, a risk of debts abroad, a risk of a market, and a risk of his factor, and has a risk of a market to come, and therefore ought to have an answerable profit.

Thirdly, if it has been a trading voyage, perhaps the adventurer has paid three or four such premiums, which sometimes make the insurer clear more by a voyage than the merchant. I myself have paid 100 pounds insurances in those small premiums on a voyage I have not gotten 50 pounds by; and I suppose I am not the first that has done so either.

This way of assuring has also, as other arts of trade have, suffered some improvement (if I may be allowed that term) in our age; and the first step upon it was an insurance office for houses, to insure them from fire. Common fame gives the project to Dr. Barebone - a man, I suppose, better known as a builder than a physician. Whether it were his, or whose it was, I do not inquire; it was settled on a fund of ground rents, to answer in case of loss, and met with very good acceptance.

But it was soon followed by another, by way of friendly society, where all who subscribe pay their quota to build up any man's house who is a contributor, if it shall happen to be burnt. I won't decide which is the best, or which succeeded best, but I believe the latter brings in most money to the contriver.

Only one benefit I cannot omit which they reap from these two societies who are not concerned in either; that if any fire happen, whether in houses insured or not insured, they have each of them a set of lusty fellows, generally watermen, who being immediately called up, wherever they live, by watchmen appointed, are, it must be confessed, very active and diligent in helping to put out the fire.

As to any further improvement to be made upon assurances in trade, no question there may; and I doubt not but on payment of a small duty to the government the king might be made the general insurer of all foreign trade, of which more under another head.

I am of the opinion also that an office of insurance erected to insure the titles of lands, in an age where they are so precarious as now, might be a project not unlikely to succeed, if established on a good fund. But I shall say no more to that, because it seems to be a design in hand by some persons in town, and is indeed no thought of my own.

Insuring of life I cannot admire; I shall say nothing to it but that in Italy, where stabbing and poisoning is so much in vogue, something may be said for it, and on contingent annuities; and yet I never knew the thing much approved of on any account.

OF FRIENDLY SOCIETIES.

***

Another branch of insurance is by contribution, or (to borrow the term from that before mentioned) friendly societies; which is, in short, a number of people entering into a mutual compact to help one another in case any disaster or distress fall upon them.

If mankind could agree, as these might be regulated, all things which have casualty in them might be secured. But one thing is particularly required in this way of assurances: none can be admitted but such whose circumstances are (at least, in some degree) alike, and so mankind must be sorted into classes; and as their contingencies differ, every different sort may be a society upon even terms; for the circumstances of people, as to life, differ extremely by the age and constitution of their bodies and difference of employment – as he that lives on shore against him that goes to sea, or a young man against an old man, or a shopkeeper against a soldier, are unequal. I do not pretend to determine the controverted point of predestination, the foreknowledge and decrees of Providence. Perhaps, if a man be decreed to be killed in the trenches, the same foreknowledge ordered him to list himself a soldier, that it might come to pass, and the like of a seaman. But this I am sure, speaking of second causes, a seaman or a soldier are subject to more contingent hazards than other men, and therefore are not upon equal terms to form such a society; nor is an annuity on the life of such a man worth so much as it is upon other men: therefore if a society should agree together to pay the executor of every member so much after the decease of the said member, the seamen's executors would most certainly have an advantage, and receive more than they pay. So that it is necessary to sort the world into parcels – seamen with seamen, soldiers with soldiers, and the like.

Nor is this a new thing; the friendly society must not pretend to assume to themselves the contrivance of the method, or think us guilty of borrowing from them, when we draw this into other branches; for I know nothing is taken from them but the bare words, "friendly society," which they cannot pretend to be any considerable piece of invention either.

I can refer them to the very individual practice in other things, which claims prescription beyond the beginning of the last age, and that is in our marshes and fens in Essex, Kent, and the Isle of Ely; where great quantities of land being with much pains and a vast charge recovered out of the seas and rivers, and maintained with banks (which they call walls), the owners of those lands agree to contribute to the keeping up those walls and keeping out the sea, which is all one with a friendly society; and if I have a piece of land in any level or marsh, though it bounds nowhere on the sea or river, yet I pay my proportion to the maintenance of the said wall or bank; and if at any time the sea breaks in, the damage is not laid upon the man in whose land the breach happened, unless it was by his neglect, but it lies on the whole land, and is called a "level lot."

Again, I have known it practised in troops of horse, especially when it was so ordered that the troopers mounted themselves; where every private trooper has agreed to pay, perhaps, 2d. per diem out of his pay into a public stock, which stock was employed to remount any of the troop who by accident should lose his horse.

Again, the sailors' contribution to the Chest at Chatham is another friendly society, and more might be named.

To argue against the lawfulness of this would be to cry down common equity as well as charity: for as it is kind that my neighbour should relieve me if I fall into distress or decay, so it is but equal he should do so if I agreed to have done the same for him; and if God Almighty has commanded us to relieve and help one another in distress, surely it must be commendable to bind ourselves by agreement to obey that command; nay, it seems to be a project that we are led to by the divine rule, and has such a latitude in it that for aught I know, as I said, all the disasters in the world might be prevented by it, and mankind be secured from all the miseries, indigences, and distresses that happen in the world. In which I crave leave to be a little particular.

First general peace might be secured all over the world by it, if all the powers agreed to suppress him that usurped or encroached upon his neighbour. All the contingencies of life might be fenced against by this method (as fire is already), as thieves, floods by land, storms by sea, losses of all sorts, and death itself, in a manner, by making it up to the survivor.

I shall begin with the seamen; for as their lives are subject to more hazards than others, they seem to come first in view.

OF SEAMEN.

***

Sailors are les enfants perdus, "the forlorn hope of the world;" they are fellows that bid defiance to terror, and maintain a constant war with the elements; who, by the magic of their art, trade in the very confines of death, and are always posted within shot, as I may say, of the grave. It is true, their familiarity with danger makes them despise it (for which, I hope, nobody will say they are the wiser); and custom has so hardened them that we find them the worst of men, though always in view of their last moment.

I have observed one great error in the custom of England relating to these sort of people, and which this way of friendly society would be a remedy for:

If a seaman who enters himself, or is pressed into, the king's service be by any accident wounded or disabled, to recompense him for the loss, he receives a pension during life, which the sailors call "smart-money," and is proportioned to their hurt, as for the loss of an eye, arm, leg, or finger, and the like: and as it is a very honourable thing, so it is but reasonable that a poor man who loses his limbs (which are his estate) in the service of the Government, and is thereby disabled from his labour to get his bread, should be provided for, and not suffer to beg or starve for want of those limbs he lost in the service of his country.

But if you come to the seamen in the merchants' service, not the least provision is made: which has been the loss of many a good ship, with many a rich cargo, which would otherwise have been saved.

And the sailors are in the right of it, too. For instance, a merchant ship coming home from the Indies, perhaps very rich, meets with a privateer (not so strong but that she might fight him and perhaps get off); the captain calls up his crew, tells them, "Gentlemen, you see how it is; I don't question but we may clear ourselves of this caper, if you will stand by me." One of the crew, as willing to fight as the rest, and as far from a coward as the captain, but endowed with a little more wit than his fellows, replies, "Noble captain, we are all willing to fight, and don't question but to beat him off; but here is the case: if we are taken, we shall be set on shore and then sent home, and lose perhaps our clothes and a little pay; but if we fight and beat the privateer, perhaps half a score of us may be wounded and lose our limbs, and then we are undone and our families. If you will sign an obligation to us that the owners or merchants shall allow a pension to such as are maimed, that we may not fight for the ship, and go a begging ourselves, we will bring off the ship or sink by her side; otherwise I am not willing to fight, for my part." The captain cannot do this; so they strike, and the ship and cargo are lost.

If I should turn this supposed example into a real history, and name the ship and the captain that did so, it would be too plain to be contradicted.

Wherefore, for the encouragement of sailors in the service of the merchant, I would have a friendly society erected for seamen; wherein all sailors or seafaring men, entering their names, places of abode, and the voyages they go upon at an office of insurance for seamen, and paying there a certain small quarterage of 1s. per quarter, should have a sealed certificate from the governors of the said office for the articles hereafter mentioned:

I.

If any such seaman, either in fight or by any other accident at sea, come to be disabled, he should receive from the said office the following sums of money, either in pension for life, or ready money, as he pleased:

For the loss of	Pounds	or Pounds (per annum for life)
An eye	25	2
Both eyes	100	8
One leg	50	4
Both legs	80	6
Right hand	80	6
Left hand	50	4
Right arm	100	8
Left arm	80	6
Both hands	160	12
Both arms	200	16

Any broken arm, or leg, or thigh, towards the cure 10 pounds If taken by the Turks, 50 pounds towards his ransom. If he become infirm and unable to go to sea or maintain himself by age or sickness 6 pounds per annum. To their wives if they are killed or drowned 50 pounds

In consideration of this, every seaman subscribing to the society shall agree to pay to the receipt of the said office his quota of the sum to be paid whenever, and as often as, such claims are made, the claims to be entered into the office and upon sufficient proof made, the governors to regulate the division and publish it in print.

For example, suppose 4,000 seamen subscribe to this society, and after six months – for no man should claim sooner than six months – a merchant's ship having engaged a privateer, there comes several claims together, as thus–

	Pounds
A was wounded and lost one leg	50
B blown up with powder, and has lost an eye	25
had a great shot took off his arm	100
D with a splinter had an eye struck out	25
E was killed with a great shot; to be paid to his wife	50
	===
	250

The governors hereupon settle the claims of these persons, and make publication "that whereas such and such seamen, members of the society, have in an engagement with a French privateer been so and so hurt, their claims upon the office, by the rules and agreement of the said office, being adjusted by the governors, amounts to 250 pounds, which, being equally divided among the subscribers, comes to 1s. 3d. each, which all persons that are subscribers to the said office are desired to pay in for their respective subscriptions, that the said wounded persons may be relieved accordingly, as they expect to be relieved if the same or the like casualty should befall them."

It is but a small matter for a man to contribute, if he gave 1s. 3d. out of his wages to relieve five wounded men of his own fraternity; but at the same time to be assured that if he is hurt or maimed he shall have the same relief, is a thing so rational that hardly anything but a harebrained follow, that thinks of nothing, would omit entering himself into such an office.

I shall not enter further into this affair, because perhaps I may give the proposal to some persons who may set it on foot, and then the world may see the benefit of it by the execution.

II. – FOR WIDOWS.

The same method of friendly society, I conceive, would be a very proper proposal for widows.

We have abundance of women, who have been bred well and lived well, ruined in a few years, and perhaps left young with a houseful of children and nothing to support them, which falls generally upon the wives of the inferior clergy, or of shopkeepers and artificers.

They marry wives with perhaps 300 pounds to 1,000 pounds portion, and can settle no jointure upon them. Either they are extravagant and idle, and waste it; or trade decays; or losses or a thousand contingencies happen to bring a tradesman to poverty, and he breaks. The poor young woman, it may be, has three or four children, and is driven to a thousand shifts, while he lies in the Mint or Friars under the dilemma of a statute of bankruptcy; but if he dies, then she is absolutely undone, unless she has friends to go to.

Suppose an office to be erected, to be called an office of insurance for widows, upon the following conditions:

Two thousand women, or their husbands for them, enter their names into a register to be kept for that purpose, with the names, age, and trade of their husbands, with the place of their abode, paying at the time of their entering 5s. down with 1s. 4d. per quarter, which is to the setting up and support of an office with clerks and all proper officers for the same; for there is no maintaining such without charge. They receive every one of them a certificate sealed by the secretary of the office, and signed by the governors, for the articles hereafter mentioned:

If any one of the women become a widow at any time after six months from the date of her subscription, upon due notice given, and claim made at the office in form as shall be directed, she shall receive within six mouths after such claim made the sum of 500 pounds in money without any deductions, saving some small fees to the officers, which the trustees must settle, that they may be known.

In consideration of this, every woman so subscribing obliges herself to pay, as often as any member of the society becomes a widow, the due proportion or share, allotted to her to pay towards the 500 pounds for the said widow, provided her share does not exceed the sum of 5s.

No seamen's or soldiers' wives to be accepted into such a proposal as this, on the account before mentioned, because the contingencies of their lives are not equal to others – unless they will admit this general exception, supposing they do not die out of the kingdom.

It might also be an exception that if the widow that claimed had really, bona fide, left her by her husband to her own use, clear of all debts and legacies, 2,000 pounds, she should have no claim, the intent being to aid the poor, not add to the rich. But there lie a great many objections against such an article, as–

1. It may tempt some to forswear themselves.

2. People will order their wills so as to defraud the exception.

One exception must be made, and that is, either very unequal matches (as when a woman of nineteen marries an old man of seventy), or women who have infirm husbands – I mean, known and publicly so; to remedy which two things are to be done:

1. The office must have moving officers without doors, who shall inform themselves of such matters, and if any such circumstances appear, the office should have fourteen days' time to return their money and declare their subscriptions void.

2. No woman whose husband had any visible distemper should claim under a year after her subscription.

One grand objection against this proposal is, how you will oblige people to pay either their subscription or their quarterage.

To this I answer, by no compulsion (though that might be performed too), but altogether voluntary; only with this argument to move it, that if they do not continue their payments, they lose the benefit of their past contributions.

I know it lies as a fair objection against such a project as this, that the number of claims are so uncertain that nobody knows what they engage in when they subscribe, for so many may die annually out of two thousand as may make my payment 20 pounds or 25 pounds per annum; and if a woman happen to pay that for twenty years, though she receives the 500 pounds at last, she is a great loser; but if she dies before her husband, she has lessened his estate considerably, and brought a great loss upon him.

First, I say to this that I would have such a proposal as this be so fair and so easy, that if any person who had subscribed found the payments too high and the claims fall too often, it should be at their liberty at any time, upon notice given, to be released, and stand obliged no longer; and, if so, volenti non fit injuria. Every one knows best what their own circumstances will bear.

In the next place, because death is a contingency no man can directly calculate, and all that subscribe must take the hazard; yet that a prejudice against this notion may not be built on wrong grounds, let us examine a little the probable hazard, and see how many shall die annually out of 2,000 subscribers, accounting by the common proportion of burials to the number of the living.

Sir William Petty, in his political arithmetic, by a very ingenious calculation, brings the account of burials in London to be one in forty annually, and proves it by all the proper rules of proportioned computation; and I will take my scheme from thence.

If, then, one in forty of all the people in England die, that supposes fifty to die every year out of our two thousand subscribers; and for a woman to contribute 5s. to every one, would certainly be to agree to pay 12 pounds 10s. per annum. upon her husband's life, to receive 500 pounds when he died, and lose it if she died first; and yet this would not be a hazard beyond reason too great for the gain.

But I shall offer some reasons to prove this to be impossible in our case: first, Sir William Petty allows the city of London to contain about a million of people, and our yearly bill of mortality never yet amounted to 25,000 in the most sickly years we have had (plague years excepted); sometimes but to 20,000, which is but one in fifty. Now it is to be considered here that children and ancient people make up, one time with another, at least one-third of our bills of mortality, and our assurances lie upon none but the middling age of the people, which is the only age wherein life is anything steady; and if that be allowed, there cannot die by his computation above one in eighty of such people every year; but because I would be sure to leave room for casualty, I will allow one in fifty shall die out of our number subscribed.

Secondly, it must be allowed that our payments falling due only on the death of husbands, this one in fifty must not be reckoned upon the two thousand, for it is to be supposed at least as many women shall die as men, and then there is nothing to pay; so that one in fifty upon one thousand is the most that I can suppose shall claim the contribution in a year, which is twenty claims a year at 5s. each, and is 5 pounds per annum. And if a woman pays this for twenty years, and claims at last, she is gainer enough, and no extraordinary loser if she never claims at all. And

I verily believe any office might undertake to demand at all adventures not above 6 pounds per annum, and secure the subscriber 500 pounds in case she come to claim as a widow.

I forbear being more particular on this thought, having occasion to be larger in other prints, the experiment being resolved upon by some friends who are pleased to think this too useful a project not to be put in execution, and therefore I refer the reader to the public practice of it.

I have named these two cases as special experiments of what might be done by assurances in way of friendly society; and I believe I might, without arrogance, affirm that the same thought might be improved into methods that should prevent the general misery and poverty of mankind, and at once secure us against beggars, parish poor, almshouses, and hospitals; and by which not a creature so miserable or so poor but should claim subsistence as their due, and not ask it of charity.

I cannot believe any creature so wretchedly base as to beg of mere choice, but either it must proceed from want or sordid prodigious covetousness; and thence I affirm there can be no beggar but he ought to be either relieved or punished, or both. If a man begs for more covetousness without want, it is a baseness of soul so extremely sordid as ought to be used with the utmost contempt, and punished with the correction due to a dog. If he begs for want, that want is procured by slothfulness and idleness, or by accident; if the latter, he ought to be relieved; if the former, he ought to be punished for the cause, but at the same time relieved also, for no man ought to starve, let his crime be what it will.

I shall proceed, therefore, to a scheme by which all mankind, be he never so mean, so poor, so unable, shall gain for himself a just claim to a comfortable subsistence whosoever age or casualty shall reduce him to a necessity of making use of it. There is a poverty so far from being despicable that it is honourable, when a man by direct casualty, sudden Providence, and without any procuring of his own, is reduced to want relief from others, as by fire, shipwreck, loss of limbs, and the like.

These are sometimes so apparent that they command the charity of others; but there are also many families reduced to decay whose conditions are not so public, and yet their necessities as great. Innumerable circumstances reduce men to want; and pressing poverty obliges some people to make their cases public, or starve; and from thence came the custom of begging, which sloth and idleness has improved into a trade. But the method I propose, thoroughly put in practice, would remove the cause, and the effect would cease of course.

Want of consideration is the great reason why people do not provide in their youth and strength for old age and sickness; and the ensuing proposal is, in short, only this that all persons in the time of their health and youth, while they are able to work and spare it, should lay up some small inconsiderable part of their gettings as a deposit in safe hands, to lie as a store in bank to relieve them, if by age or accident they come to be disabled, or incapable to provide for themselves; and that if God so bless them that they nor theirs never come to need it, the overplus may be employed to relieve such as shall.

If an office in the same nature with this were appointed in every county in England, I doubt not but poverty might easily be prevented, and begging wholly suppressed

THE PROPOSAL IS FOR A PENSION OFFICE.

That an office be erected in some convenient place, where shall be a secretary, a clerk, and a searcher, always attending.

That all sorts of people who are labouring people and of honest repute, of what calling or condition soever, men or women (beggars and soldiers excepted), who, being sound of their limbs and under fifty years of age, shall come to the said office and enter their names, trades, and places of abode into a register to be kept for that purpose, and shall pay down at the time of the said entering the sum of sixpence, and from thence one shilling per quarter, shall every one have an assurance under the seal of the said office for these following conditions:

1. Every such subscriber, if by any casualty (drunkenness and quarrels excepted) they break their

limbs, dislocate joints, or are dangerously maimed or bruised, able surgeons appointed for that purpose shall take them into their care, and endeavour their cure gratis.

2. If they are at any time dangerously sick, on notice given to the said office able physicians shall be appointed to visit them, and give their prescriptions gratis.

3. If by sickness or accident, as aforesaid, they lose their limbs or eyes, so as to be visibly disabled to work, and are otherwise poor and unable to provide for themselves, they shall either be cured at the charge of the office, or be allowed a pension for subsistence during life.

4. If they become lame, aged, bedrid, or by real infirmity of body are unable to work, and otherwise incapable to provide for themselves, on proof made that it is really and honestly so they shall be taken into a college or hospital provided for that purpose, and be decently maintained during life.

5. If they are seamen, and die abroad on board the merchants' ships they were employed in, or are cast away and drowned, or taken and die in slavery, their widows shall receive a pension during their widowhood.

6. If they were tradesmen and paid the parish rates, if by decay and failure of trade they break and are put in prison for debt, they shall receive a pension for subsistence during close imprisonment.

7. If by sickness or accidents they are reduced to extremities of poverty for a season, on a true representation to the office they shall be relieved as the governors shall see cause.

It is to be noted that in the fourth article such as by sickness and age are disabled from work, and poor, shall be taken into the house and provided for; whereas in the third article they who are blind or have lost limbs, shall have pensions allowed them.

The reason of this difference is this:

A poor man or woman that has lost his hand, or leg, or sight, is visibly disabled, and we cannot be deceived; whereas other infirmities are not so easily judged of, and everybody would be claiming a pension, when but few will demand being taken into a hospital but such as are really in want.

And that this might be managed with such care and candour as a design which carries so good a face ought to be, I propose the following method for putting it into practice:

I suppose every undertaking of such a magnitude must have some principal agent to push it forward, who must manage and direct everything, always with direction of the governors.

And first I will suppose one general office erected for the great parishes of Stepney and Whitechapel; and as I shall lay down afterwards some methods to oblige all people to come in and subscribe, so I may be allowed to suppose here that all the inhabitants of those two large parishes (the meaner labouring sort,

I mean) should enter their names, and that the number of them should be 100,000, as I believe they would be at least.

First, there should be named fifty of the principal inhabitants of the said parishes (of which the churchwardens for the time being, and all the justices of the peace dwelling in the bounds of the said parish, and the ministers resident for the time being, to be part) to be governors of the said office.

The said fifty to be first nominated by the Lord Mayor of London for the time being, and every vacancy to be supplied in ten days at farthest by the majority of voices of the rest.

The fifty to choose a committee of eleven, to sit twice a week, of whom three to be a quorum; with a chief governor, a deputy-governor, and a treasurer.

In the office, a secretary with clerks of his own, a registrar and two clerks, four searchers, a messenger (one in daily attendance under salary), a physician, a surgeon, and four visitors.

In the hospital, more or less (according to the number of people entertained), a housekeeper, a steward, nurses, a porter, and a chaplain.

For the support of this office, and that the deposit money might go to none but the persons and uses for whom it is paid, and that it might not be said officers and salaries was the chief end of the undertaking (as in many a project it has been), I propose that the manager or undertaker, whom I mentioned before, be the secretary, who shall have a clerk allowed him, whose business it shall be to keep the register, take the entries, and give out the tickets (sealed by the governors and signed by himself), and to enter always the payment of quarterage of every subscriber. And that there may be no fraud or connivance, and too great trust be not reposed in the said secretary, every subscriber who brings his quarterage is to put it into a great chest, locked up with eleven locks, every member of the committee to keep a key, so that it cannot be opened but in the presence of them all; and every time a subscriber pays his quarterage, the secretary shall give him a sealed ticket thus [Christmas 96] which shall be allowed as the receipt of quarterage for that quarter.

> Note. – The reason why every subscriber shall take a receipt or ticket for his quarterage is because this must be the standing law of the office – that if any subscribers fail to pay their quarterage, they shall never claim after it until double so much be paid, nor not at all that quarter, whatever befalls them.

The secretary should be allowed to have 2d. for every ticket of entry he gives out, and ld. for every receipt he gives for quarterage, to be accounted for as follows:

One-third to himself in lieu of salary, he being to pay three clerks out of it.

One-third to the clerks and other officers among them.

And one-third to defray the incident charge of the office.

Thus calculated.		Per annum.
		Pounds s. d.
100,000 subscribers paying 1d. each every quarter		1,666 3 4
One-third	To the secretary per annum and three clerks	555 7 9
		Pounds per annum.
One-third	{ To a registrar 100 }	550 0 0
	{ To a clerk 50 }	
	{ To four searchers 100 }	
	{ To a physician 100 }	
	{ To a surgeon 100 }	
	{ To four visitors 100 }	
One-third to incident charges, such as	{ To ten committee-men, 5s. each sitting, twice per week is 260 }	560 15 7
	{ To a clerk of committees 50 }	
	{ To a messenger 40 }	
	{ A house for the office 40 }	
	{ A house for the }	
	{ hospital 100 }	
	{ Contingencies 70 }	
	15s. 7d.	===============
		1,666 3 4

All the charge being thus paid out of such a trifle as ld. per quarter, the next consideration is to examine what the incomes of this subscription may be, and in time what may be the demands upon it.

	Pounds s. d.
If 100,000 persons subscribe, they pay down at their entering each 6d., which is	2,500 0 0
And the first year's payment is in stock at 1s. per quarter	20,000 0 0
It must be allowed that under three months the subscriptions will not be well complete; so the payment of quarterage shall not begin but from the day after the books are full, or shut up; and from thence one year is to pass before any claim can be made; and the money coming in at separate times, I suppose no improvement upon it for the first year, except of the 2,500 pounds, which, lent to the king on some good fund at 7 pounds per cent. interest, advances the first year	175 0 0
The quarterage of the second year, abating for 1,000 claims	19,800 0 0
And the interest of the first year's money at the end of the second year, lent to the king, as aforesaid, at 7 per cent. interest, is	1,774 10 0
The quarterage of the third year, abating for claims	19,400 0 0
The interest of former cash to the end of the third year	3,284 8 0

	==============
Income of three years	66,933 18 0

Note. - Any persons may pay 2s. up to 5s. quarterly, if they please, and upon a claim will be allowed in proportion.

To assign what shall be the charge upon this, where contingency has so great a share, is not to be done; but by way of political arithmetic a probable guess may be made.

It is to be noted that the pensions I propose to be paid to persons claiming by the third, fifth, and sixth articles are thus: every person who paid 1s. quarterly shall receive 12d. weekly, and so in proportion every 12d. paid quarterly by any one person to receive so many shillings weekly, if they come to claim a pension.

The first year no claim is allowed; so the bank has in stock completely 22,500 pounds. From thence we are to consider the number of claims.

Sir William Petty, in his "Political Arithmetic," supposes not above one in forty to die per annum out of the whole number of people; and I can by no means allow that the circumstances of our claims will be as frequent as death, for these reasons:

1. Our subscriptions respect all persons grown and in the prime of their age; past the first, and providing against the last, part of danger (Sir William's account including children and old people, which always make up one-third of the bills of mortality).

2. Our claims will fall thin at first for several years; and let but the money increase for ten years, as it does in the account for three years, it would be almost sufficient to maintain the whole number.

3. Allow that casualty and poverty are our debtor side; health, prosperity, and death are the creditor side of the account; and in all probable accounts those three articles will carry off three fourth-parts of the number, as follows: If one in forty shall die annually (as no doubt they shall, and more), that is 2,500 a year, which in twenty years is 50,000 of the number; I hope I may be allowed one-third to be out of condition to claim, apparently living without the help of charity, and one third in health and body, and able to work; which, put together, make 83,332; so it leaves 16,668 to make claims of charity and pensions in the first twenty years, and one-half of them must, according to Sir William Petty, die on our hands in twenty years; so there remains but 8,334.

But to put it out of doubt, beyond the proportion to be guessed at, I will allow they shall fall thus:

The first year, we are to note, none can claim; and the second year the number must be very few, but increasing: wherefore I suppose

	Pounds
One in every 500 shall claim the second year, which is 200; the charge whereof is	500
One in every 100 the third year is 1,000; the charge	2,500
Together with the former 200	500

	======
	3,500

To carry on the calculation.

	Pounds s. d.
We find the stock at the end of the third year	66,933 18 0
The quarterage of the fourth year, abating as before	19,000 0 0
Interest of the stock	4,882 17 6
The quarterage of the fifth year	18,600 0 0
Interest of the stock	6,473 0 0
	=================
	115,889 15 6
The charge	3,000 0 0
2,000 to fall the fourth year	5,000 0 0
And the old continued	3,500 0 0
2,000 the fifth year	5,000 0 0
The old continued	11,000 0 0
	================
	27,500 0 0

By this computation the stock is increased above the charge in five years 89,379 pounds 15s. 6d.; and yet here are sundry articles to be considered on both sides of the account that will necessarily increase the stock and diminish the charge:

First, in the five years' time 6,200 having claimed charity, the number being abated for in the reckoning above for stock, it may be allowed new subscriptions will be taken in to keep the number full, which in five years amounts to	3,400 0 0
Their sixpences is	115 0 0
	===============
	3,555 0 0
Which added to 115,889 pounds 15s. 6d. augments be stock to	119,444 15 6
Six thousand two hundred persons claiming help, which falls, to be sure, on the aged and infirm, I think, at a modest computation, in five years' time 500 of them may be dead, which, without allowing annually, we take at an abatement of 4,000 pounds out of the charge	4,000 0 0
Which reduces the charge to	23,500 0 0

Besides this, the interest of the quarterage, which is supposed in the former account to lie dead till the year is out, which cast up from quarter to quarter, allowing it to be put out quarterly, as it may well be, amounts to, by computation for five years, 5,250 pounds.

From the fifth year, as near as can be computed, the number of pensioners being so great, I make no doubt but they shall die off the hands of the undertaker as fast as they shall fall in, excepting, so much difference as the payment of every year, which the interest of the stock shall supply.

For example:	Pounds s. d.
At the end of the fifth year the stock in hand	94,629 15 6
The payment of the sixth year	20,000 0 0
Interest of the stock	5,408 4 0
	===================
	120,037 19 6
Allow an overplus charge for keeping in the house, which will be dearer than pensions, 10,000 pounds per annum	10,000 0 0
Charge of the sixth year	22,500 0 0
Balance in cash	87,537 19 6
	===================
	120,037 19 6

This also is to be allowed – that all those persons who are kept by the office in the house shall have employment provided for them, whereby no persons shall be kept idle, the works to be suited to every one's capacity without rigour, only some distinction to those who are most willing to work; the profits of the said work to the stock of the house.

Besides this, there may great and very profitable methods be found out to improve the stock beyond the settled interest of 7 per cent., which perhaps may not always be to be had, for the

Exchequer is not always borrowing money; but a bank of 80,000 pounds, employed by faithful hands, need not want opportunities of great, and very considerable improvement.

Also it would be a very good object for persons who die rich to leave legacies to, which in time might be very well supposed to raise a standing revenue to it.

I will not say but various contingencies may alter the charge of this undertaking, and swell the claims beyond proportion further than I extend it; but all that, and much more, is sufficiently answered in the calculations by above 80,000 pounds in stock to provide for it.

As to the calculation being made on a vast number of subscribers, and more than, perhaps, will be allowed likely to subscribe, I think the proportion may hold good in a few as well as in a great many; and perhaps if 20,000 subscribed, it might be as effectual. I am indeed willing to think all men should have sense enough to see the usefulness of such a design, and be persuaded by their interest to engage in it; but some men have less prudence than brutes, and will make no provision against age till it comes; and to deal with such, two ways might be used by authority to compel them.

1. The churchwardens and justices of peace should send the beadle of the parish, with an officer belonging to this office, about to the poorer

parishioners to tell them that, since such honourable provision is made for them to secure themselves in old age from poverty and distress, they should expect no relief from the parish if they refused to enter themselves, and by sparing so small a part of their earnings to prevent future misery.

2. The churchwardens of every parish might refuse the removal of persons and families into their parish but upon their having entered into this office.

3. All persons should be publicly desired to forbear giving anything to beggars, and all common beggars suppressed after a certain time; for this would effectually suppress beggary at last.

And, to oblige the parishes to do this on behalf of such a project, the governor of the house should secure the parish against all charges coming upon them from any person who did subscribe and pay the quarterage, and that would most certainly oblige any parish to endeavour that all the labouring meaner people in the parish should enter their names; for in time it would most certainly take all the poor in the parish off of their hands.

I know that by law no parish can refuse to relieve any person or family fallen into distress; and therefore to send them word they must expect no relief, would seem a vain threatening. But thus far the parish may do: they shall be esteemed as persons who deserve no relief, and shall be used accordingly; for who indeed would ever pity that man in his distress who at the expense of two pots of beer a month might have prevented it, and would not spare it?

As to my calculations, on which I do not depend either, I say this: if they are probable, and that in five years' time a subscription of a hundred thousand persons would have 87,537 pounds 19s. 6d. in cash, all charges paid, I desire any one but to reflect what will not such a sum do. For instance, were it laid out in the Million Lottery tickets, which are now sold at 6 pounds each, and bring in 1 pound per annum for fifteen years, every 1,000 pounds so laid out pays back in time 2,500 pounds, and that time would be as fast as it would be wanted, and therefore be as good as money; or if laid out in improving rents, as ground-rents with buildings to devolve in time, there is no question but a revenue would be raised in time to maintain one-third part of the number of subscribers, if they should come to claim charity.

And I desire any man to consider the present state of this kingdom, and tell me, if all the people of England, old and young, rich and poor, were to pay into one common bank 4s. per annum a head, and that 4s. duly and honestly managed, whether the overplus paid by those who die off, and by those who never come to want, would not in all probability maintain all that should be poor, and for ever banish beggary and poverty out of the kingdom.

OF WAGERING.

***

Wagering, as now practised by politics and contracts, is become a branch of assurances; it was before more properly a part of gaming, and as it deserved, had but a very low esteem; but shifting sides, and the war providing proper subjects, as the contingencies of sieges, battles, treaties, and campaigns, it increased to an extraordinary reputation, and offices were erected on purpose which managed it to a strange degree and with great advantage, especially to the office-keepers; so that, as has been computed, there was not less gaged on one side and other, upon the second siege of Limerick, than two hundred thousand pounds.

How it is managed, and by what trick and artifice it became a trade, and how insensibly men were drawn into it, an easy account may be given.

I believe novelty was the first wheel that set it on work, and I need make no reflection upon the power of that charm: it was wholly a new thing, at least upon the Exchange of London; and the first occasion that gave it a room among public discourse, was some persons forming wagers on the return and success of King James, for which the Government took occasion to use them as they deserved.

I have heard a bookseller in King James's time say, "That if he would have a book sell, he would have it burnt by the hand of the common hangman;" the man, no doubt, valued his profit above his reputation; but people are so addicted to prosecute a thing that seems forbid, that this very practice seemed to be encouraged by its being contraband.

The trade increased, and first on the Exchange and then in coffeehouses it got life, till the brokers, those vermin of trade, got hold of it, and then particular offices were set apart for it, and an incredible resort thither was to be seen every day.

These offices had not been long in being, but they were thronged with sharpers and setters as much as the groom-porters, or any gaming-ordinary in town, where a man had nothing to do but to make a good figure and prepare the keeper of the office to give him a credit as a good man, and though he had not a groat to pay, he should take guineas and sign polities, till he had received, perhaps, 300 pounds or 400 pounds in money, on condition to pay great odds, and then success tries the man; if he wins his fortune is made; if not, he's a better man than he was before by just so much money, for as to the debt, he is your humble servant in the Temple or Whitehall.

But besides those who are but the thieves of the trade, there is a method as effectual to get money as possible, managed with more appearing honesty, but no less art, by which the wagerer, in confederacy with the office-keeper, shall lay vast sums, great odds, and yet be always sure to win.

For example: A town in Flanders, or elsewhere, during the war is besieged; perhaps at the beginning of the siege the defence is vigorous, and relief probable, and it is the opinion of most people the town will hold out so long, or perhaps not be taken at all: the wagerer has two or three more of his sort in conjunction, of which always the office-keeper is one; and they run down all discourse of the taking the town, and offer great odds it shall not be taken by such a day. Perhaps this goes on a week, and then the scale turns; and though they seem to hold the same opinion still, yet underhand the office-keeper has orders to take all the odds which by their example was before given against the taking the town; and so all their first-given odds are easily secured, and yet the people brought into a vein of betting against the siege of the town too. Then they order all the odds to be taken as long as they will run, while they themselves openly give odds, and sign polities, and oftentimes take their own money, till they have received perhaps double what they at first laid. Then they turn the scale at once, and cry down the town, and lay that it shall be taken, till the length of the first odds is fully run; and by this manage, if the town be taken they win perhaps two or three thousand pounds, and if it be not taken, they are no losers neither.

It is visible by experience, not one town in ten is besieged but it is taken. The art of war is so improved, and our generals are so wary, that an army seldom attempts a siege, but when they are almost sure to go on with it; and no town can hold out if a relief cannot be had from abroad.

Now, if I can by first laying 500 pounds to 200 pounds with A, that the town shall not be taken, wheedle in B to lay me 5,000 pounds to 2,000 pounds of the same; and after that, by bringing down the vogue of the siege, reduce the wagers to even-hand, and lay 2,000 pounds with C that the town shall not be taken; by this method, it is plain–

If the town be not taken, I win 2,200 pounds and lose 2,000 pounds. If the town be taken, I win 5,000 pounds and lose 2,500 pounds.

This is gaming by rule, and in such a knot it is impossible to lose; for if it is in any man's or company of men's power, by any artifice to alter the odds, it is in their power to command the money out of every man's pocket, who has no more wit than to venture

OF FOOLS.

***

Of all persons who are objects of our charity, none move my compassion like those whom it has pleased God to leave in a full state health and strength, but deprived of reason to act for themselves. And it is, in my opinion, one of the greatest scandals upon the understanding of others to mock at those who want it. Upon this account I think the hospital we call Bedlam to be a noble foundation, a visible instance of the sense our ancestors had of the greatest unhappiness which can befall humankind; since as the soul in man distinguishes him from a brute, so where the soul is dead (for so it is as to acting) no brute so much a beast as a man. But since never to have it, and to have lost it, are synonymous in the effect, I wonder how it came to pass that in the settlement of that hospital they made no provision for persons born without the use of their reason, such as we call fools, or, more properly, naturals.

We use such in England with the last contempt, which I think is a strange error, since though they are useless to the commonwealth, they are only so by God's direct providence, and no previous fault.

I think it would very well become this wise age to take care of such; and perhaps they are a particular rent-charge on the great family of mankind, left by the Maker of us all, like a younger brother, who though the estate be given from him, yet his father expected the heir should take some care of him.

If I were to be asked, Who ought in particular to be charged with this work? I would answer in general those who have a portion of understanding extraordinary. Not that I would lay a tax upon any man's brains, or discourage wit by appointing wise men to maintain fools; but, some tribute is due to God's goodness for bestowing extraordinary gifts; and who can it be better paid to than such as suffer for want of the same bounty?

For the providing, therefore, some subsistence for such that natural defects may not be exposed:

It is proposed that a fool-house be erected, either by public authority, or by the city, or by an Act of Parliament, into which all that are naturals or born fools, without respect or distinction, should be admitted and maintained.

For the maintenance of this, a small stated contribution, settled by the authority of an Act of Parliament, without any damage to the persons paying the same, might be very easily raised by a tax upon learning, to be paid by the authors of books:

First, in the five years' time 6,200 having claimed charity, the number being abated for in the reckoning above for stock, it may be allowed	3,400 0 0
new subscriptions will be taken in to keep the number full, which in five years amounts to	

Every book that shall be printed in folio, from 40 sheets and upwards, to pay at the licensing (for the whole impression)	5 pounds
Under 40 sheets	40s
Every quarto	20s
Every octavo of 10 sheets and upward	20s
Every octavo under 10 sheets, and every bound book in 12mo	10s
Every stitched pamphlet	2s
Reprinted copies the same rates.	

This tax to be paid into the Chamber of London for the space of twenty years, would, without question, raise a fund sufficient to build and purchase a settlement for this house.

I suppose this little tax being to be raised at so few places as the printing-presses, or the licensers of books, and consequently the charge but very small in gathering, might bring in about 1,500 pounds per annum for the term of twenty years, which would perform the work to the degree following:

The house should be plain and decent (for I don't think the ostentation of buildings necessary or suitable to works of charity), and be built somewhere out of town for the sake of the air.

The building to cost about 1,000 pounds, or, if the revenue exceed, to cost 2,000 pounds at most, and the salaries mean in proportion.

In the House.	Per annum.

A steward	30 pounds
A purveyor	20
A cook	20
A butler	20
Six women to assist the cook and clean the house, 4 pounds each	24
Six nurses to tend the people, 3 pounds each	18
A chaplain	20
	====
	152
A hundred alms-people at 8 pounds per annum, diet, &c.	800
	====
	952
The table for the officers, and contingencies, and clothes for the alms-people, and firing, put together	500
An auditor of the accounts, a committee of the governors, and two clerks.	

Here I suppose 1,500 pounds per annum revenue, to be settled upon the house, which, it is very probable might be raised from the tax aforesaid. But since an Act of Parliament is necessary to be had for the collecting this duty, and that taxes for keeping of fools would be difficultly obtained, while they are so much wanted for wise men, I would propose to raise the money by voluntary charity, which would be a work that would leave more honour to the undertakers than feasts and great shows, which our public bodies too much diminish their stocks with.

But to pass all suppositious ways, which are easily thought of, but hardly procured, I propose to maintain fools out of our own folly. And whereas a great deal of money has been thrown about in lotteries, the following proposal would very easily perfect our work.

A CHARITY-LOTTERY.

***

That a lottery be set up by the authority of the Lord Mayor and Court of Aldermen, for a hundred thousand tickets, at twenty shillings each, to be drawn by the known way and method of drawing lotteries, as the million-lottery was drawn, in which no allowance to be made to anybody, but the fortunate to receive the full sum of one hundred thousand pounds put in, without discount, and yet this double advantage to follow:

1. That an immediate sum of one hundred thousand pounds shall be raised and paid into the Exchequer for the public use.

2. A sum of above twenty thousand pounds be gained, to be put into the hands of known trustees, to be laid out in a charity for the maintenance of the poor.

That as soon as the money shall be come in, it shall be paid into the Exchequer, either on some good fund, if any suitable, or on the credit of the Exchequer; and that when the lottery is drawn, the fortunate to receive tallies or bills from the Exchequer for their money, payable at four years.

The Exchequer receives this money, and gives out tallies according to the prizes, when it is drawn, all payable at four years; and the interest of this money for four years is struck in tallies proportioned to the maintenance; which no parish would refuse that subsisted them wholly before.

I make no question but that if such a hospital was erected within a mile or two of the city, one great circumstance would happen, viz., that the common sort of people, who are very much addicted to rambling in the fields, would make this house the customary walk, to divert themselves with the objects to be seen there, and to make what they call sport with the calamity of others, as is now shamefully allowed in Bedlam.

To prevent this, and that the condition of such, which deserves pity, not contempt, might not be the more exposed by this charity, it should be ordered: that the steward of the house be in commission of the peace within the precincts of the house only, and authorised to punish by limited fines or otherwise any person that shall offer any abuse to the poor alms-people, or shall offer to make sport at their condition.

If any person at reading of this should be so impertinent as to ask to what purpose I would appoint a chaplain in a hospital of fools, I could answer him very well by saying, for the use of the other persons, officers, and attendants in the house. But besides that, pray, why not a chaplain for fools, as well as for knaves, since both, though in a different manner, are incapable of reaping any benefit by religion, unless by some invisible influence they are made docile; and since the same secret power can restore these to their reason, as must make the other sensible, pray why not a chaplain? Idiots indeed were denied the communion in the primitive churches, but I never read they were not to be prayed for, or were not admitted to hear.

If we allow any religion, and a Divine Supreme Power, whose influence works invisibly on the hearts of men (as he must be worse than the people we talk of, who denies it), we must allow at the same time that Power can restore the reasoning faculty to an idiot, and it is our part to use the proper means of supplicating Heaven to that end, leaving the disposing part to the issue of unalterable Providence.

The wisdom of Providence has not left us without examples of some of the most stupid natural idiots in the world who have been restored to their reason, or, as one would think, had reason infused after a long life of idiotism; perhaps, among other wise ends, to confute that sordid supposition that idiots have no souls.

OF BANKRUPTS.

***

This chapter has some right to stand next to that of fools, for besides the common acceptation of late, which makes every unfortunate man a fool, I think no man so much made a fool of as a bankrupt.

If I may be allowed so much liberty with our laws, which are generally good, and above all things are tempered with mercy, lenity, and freedom, this has something in it of barbarity; it gives a loose to the malice and revenge of the creditor, as well as a power to right himself, while it leaves the debtor no way to show himself honest. It contrives all the ways possible to drive the debtor to despair, and encourages no new industry, for it makes him perfectly incapable of anything but starving.

This law, especially as it is now frequently executed, tends wholly to the destruction of the debtor, and yet very little to the advantage of the creditor.

1. The severities to the debtor are unreasonable, and, if I may so say, a little inhuman, for it not only strips him of all in a moment, but renders him for ever incapable of helping himself, or relieving his family by future industry. If he escapes from prison, which is hardly done too, if he has nothing left, he must starve or live on charity; if he goes to work no man dare pay him his wages, but he shall pay it again to the creditors; if he has any private stock left for a subsistence he can put it nowhere; every man is

bound to be a thief and take it from him; if he trusts it in the hands of a friend he must receive it again as a great courtesy, for that friend is liable to account for it. I have known a poor man prosecuted by a statute to that degree that all he had left was a little money which he knew not where to hide; at last, that he might not starve, he gives it to his brother who had entertained him; the brother, after he had his money quarrels with him to get him out of his house, and when he desires him to let him have the money lent him, gives him this for answer, I cannot pay you safely, for there is a statute against you; which run the poor man to such extremities that he destroyed himself. Nothing is more frequent than for men who are reduced by miscarriage in trade to compound and set up again and get good estates; but a statute, as we call it, for ever shuts up all doors to the debtor's recovery, as if breaking were a crime so capital that he ought to be cast out of human society and exposed to extremities worse than death. And, which will further expose the fruitless severity of this law, it is easy to make it appear that all this cruelty to the debtor is so far, generally speaking, from advantaging the creditors, that it destroys the estate, consumes it in extravagant charges, and unless the debtor be consenting, seldom makes any considerable dividends. And I am bold to say there is no advantage made by the prosecuting of a statute with severity, but what might be doubly made by methods more merciful. And though I am not to prescribe to the legislators of the nation, yet by way of essay I take leave to give my opinion and my experience in the methods, consequences, and remedies of this law.

All people know, who remember anything of the times when that law was made, that the evil it was pointed at was grown very rank, and breaking to defraud creditors so much a trade, that the parliament had good reason to set up a fury to deal with it; and I am far from reflecting on the makers of that law, who, no question, saw it was necessary at that time. But as laws, though in themselves good, are more or less so, as they are more or less seasonable, squared, and adapted to the circumstances and time of the evil they are made against; so it were worth while (with submission) for the same authority to examine:

1. Whether the length of time since that act was made has not given opportunity to debtors,

(1) To evade the force of the act by ways and shifts to avoid the power of it, and secure their estates out of the reach of it.

(2) To turn the point of it against those whom it was made to relieve. Since we see frequently now that bankrupts desire statutes, and procure them to be taken out against themselves.

2. Whether the extremities of this law are not often carried on beyond the true intent and meaning of the act itself by persons who, besides being creditors, are also malicious, and gratify their private revenge by prosecuting the offender, to the ruin of his family.

If these two points are to be proved, then I am sure it will follow that this act is now a public grievance to the nation, and I doubt not but will be one time or other repealed by the same wise authority which made it.

1. Time and experience has furnished the debtors with ways and means to evade the force of this statute, and to secure their estate against the reach of it, which renders it often insignificant, and consequently, the knave against whom the law was particularly bent gets off, while he only who fails of mere necessity, and whose honest principle will not permit him to practise those methods, is exposed to the fury of this act. And as things are now ordered, nothing is more easy than for a man to order his estate so that a statute shall have no power over it, or at least but a little.

If the bankrupt be a merchant, no statute can reach his effects beyond the seas; so that he has nothing to secure but his books, and away he goes into the Friars. If a Shopkeeper, he has more difficulty: but that is made easy, for there are men and carts to be had whose trade it is, and who in one night shall remove the greatest warehouse of goods or cellar of wines in the town and carry them off into those nurseries of rogues, the Mint and Friars; and our constables and watch, who are the allowed magistrates of the night, and who shall stop a poor little lurking thief, that it may be has stole a bundle of old clothes, worth five shilling, shall let them all pass without any disturbance, and hundred honest men robbed of their estates before their faces, to the eternal infamy of the justice of the nation.

And were a man but to hear the discourse among the inhabitants of those dens of thieves, when they first swarm about a newcomer to comfort him, for they are not all hardened to a like degree at once. "Well," says the first, "come, don't be concerned, you have got a good parcel of goods away I promise you, you need not value all the world." "All! would I had done so," says another, "I'd a laughed at all my creditors." "Ay," says the young proficient in the hardened trade, "but my creditors!" "Hang the creditors!" says a third; "why, there's such a one, and such a one, they have creditors too, and they won't agree with them, and here they live like gentlemen, and care not a farthing for them. Offer your creditors half a crown in the pound, and pay it them in old debts, and if they won't take it let them alone; they'll come after you, never fear it." "Oh! but a statute," says he again. "Oh! but the devil," cries the Minter. "Why, 'tis the statutes we live by," say they; "why, if it were not for statutes, creditors would comply, and debtors would compound, and we honest fellows here of the Mint would be starved. Prithee, what need you care for a statute? A thousand statutes can't reach you here." This is the language of the country, and the newcomer soon learns to speak it; for I think I may say, without wronging any man, I have known many a man go in among them honest, that is, without ill design, but I never knew one come away so again. Then comes a graver sort among this black crew (for here, as in hell, are fiends of degrees and different magnitude), and he falls into discourse with the newcomer, and gives him more solid advice. "Look you, sir, I am concerned to see you melancholy; I am in your circumstance too, and if you'll accept of it, I'll give you the best advice I can," and so begins the grave discourse.

The man is in too much trouble not to want counsel, so he thanks him, and he goes on:- "Send a summons to your creditors, and offer them what you can propose in the pound (always reserving a good stock to begin the world again), which if they will take, you are a free man, and better than you were before; if they won't take it, you know the worst of it, you are on the better side of the hedge with them: if they will not take it, but will proceed to a statute, you have nothing to do but to oppose force with force; for the laws of nature tell you, you must not starve; and a statute is so barbarous, so unjust, so malicious a way of proceeding against a man, that I do not think any debtor obliged to consider anything but his own preservation, when once they go on with that." "For why," says the old studied wretch, "should the creditors spend your estate in the commission, and then demand the debt of you too? Do you owe anything to the commission of the statute?" "No," says he. "Why, then," says he, "I warrant their charges will come to 200 pounds out of your estate, and they must have 10s. a day for starving you and your family. I cannot see why any man should think I am bound in conscience to pay the extravagance of other men. If my creditors spend 500 pounds in getting in my estate by a statute, which I offered to surrender without it, I'll reckon that 500 pounds paid them, let them take it among them, for equity is due to a bankrupt as well as to any man, and if the laws do not give it us, we must take it."

This is too rational discourse not to please him, and he proceeds by this advice; the creditors cannot agree, but take out a statute; and the man that offered at first it may be 10s. in the pound, is kept in that cursed place till he has spent it all and can offer nothing, and then gets away beyond sea, or after a long consumption gets off by an act of relief to poor debtors, and all the charges of the statute fall among the creditors. Thus I knew a statute taken out against a shopkeeper in the country, and a considerable parcel of goods too seized, and yet the creditors, what with charges and two or three suits at law, lost their whole debts and 8s. per pound contribution money for charges, and the poor debtor, like a man under the surgeon's hand, died in the operation.

2. Another evil that time and experience has brought to light from this act is, when the debtor himself shall confederate with some particular creditor to take out a statute, and this is a masterpiece of plot and intrigue. For perhaps some creditor honestly received in the way of trade a large sum of money of

the debtor for goods sold him when he was sui juris, and he by consent shall own himself a bankrupt before that time, and the statute shall reach back to bring in an honest man's estate, to help pay a rogue's debt. Or a man shall go and borrow a sum of money upon a parcel of goods, and lay them to pledge; he keeps the money, and the statute shall fetch away the goods to help forward the composition. These are tricks I can give too good an account of, having more than once suffered by the experiment. I could give a scheme, of more ways, but I think it is needless to prove the necessity of laying aside that law, which is pernicious to both debtor and creditor, and chiefly hurtful to the honest man whom it was made to preserve.

The next inquiry is, whether the extremities of this law are not often carried on beyond the true intent and meaning of the act itself, for malicious and private ends to gratify passion and revenge?

I remember the answer a person gave me, who had taken out statutes against several persons, and some his near relations, who had failed in his debt; and when I was one time dissuading him from prosecuting a man who owed me money as well as him, I used this argument with him:- "You know the man has nothing left to pay." "That's true," says he; "I know that well enough." "To what purpose, then," said I, "will you prosecute him?" "Why, revenge is sweet," said he. Now a man that will prosecute a debtor, not as a debtor, but by way of revenge, such a man is, I think, not intentionally within the benefit of our law.

In order to state the case right, there are four sorts of people to be considered in this discourse; and the true case is how to distinguish them,

1. There is the honest debtor, who fails by visible necessity, losses, sickness, decay of trade, or the like.

2. The knavish, designing, or idle, extravagant debtor, who fails because either he has run out his estate in excesses, or on purpose to cheat and abuse his creditors.

3. There is the moderate creditor, who seeks but his own, but will omit no lawful means to gain it, and yet will hear reasonable and just arguments and proposals.

4. There is the rigorous severe creditor, that values not whether the debtor be honest man or knave, able or unable, but will have his debt, whether it be to be had or no, without mercy, without compassion, full of ill language, passion, and revenge.

How to make a law to suit to all these is the case. That a necessary favour might be shown to the first, in pity and compassion to the unfortunate, in commiseration of casualty and poverty, which no man is exempt from the danger of. That a due rigour and restraint be laid upon the second, that villainy and knavery might not be encouraged by a law. That a due care be taken of the third, that men's estates may as far as can be secured to them. And due limits set to the last, that no man may have an unlimited power over his fellow-subjects, to the ruin of both life and estate.

All which I humbly conceive might be brought to pass by the following method, to which I give the title of

A COURT OF INQUIRIES.

This court should consist of a select number of persons, to be chosen yearly out of the several wards of the City by the Lord Mayor and Court of Aldermen, and out of the several Inns of Court by the Lord Chancellor, or Lord Keeper, for the time being, and to consist of,

A President, } To be chosen by the rest, and named every year also.

A Secretary, }

A Treasurer, }

A judge of causes for the proof of debts.

Fifty-two citizens, out of every ward two; of which number to be twelve merchants.

Two lawyers (barristers at least) out of each of the Inns of Court.

That a Commission of Inquiry into bankrupts' estates be given to these, con-

firmed and settled by Act of Parliament, with power to hear, try, and determine causes as to proof of debts, and disputes in accounts between debtor and creditor, without appeal.

The office for this court to be at Guildhall, where clerks should be always attending, and a quorum of the commissioners to sit de die in diem, from three to six o'clock in the afternoon.

To this court every man who finds himself pressed by his affairs, so that he cannot carry on his business, shall apply himself as follows:-

He shall go to the secretary's office, and give in his name, with this short petition:-

> To the Honourable the President and Commissioners of His Majesty's Court of Inquiries. The humble petition of A. B., of the Parish of - in the Haberdasher.
>
> Showeth
>
> That your petitioner being unable to carry on his business, by reason of great losses and decay of trade, and being ready and willing to make a full and entire discovery of his whole estate, and to deliver up the same to your honours upon oath, as the law directs for the satisfaction of his creditors, and having to that purpose entered his name into the books of your office on the - of this instant.
>
> Your petitioner humbly prays the protection of this Honourable Court.
>
> And shall ever pray.

The secretary is to lay this petition before the commissioners, who shall sign it of course; and the petitioner shall have an officer sent home with him immediately, who shall take possession of his house and goods, and an exact inventory of everything therein shall be taken at his entrance by other officers also, appointed by the court; according to which inventory the first officer and the bankrupt also shall be accountable.

This officer shall supersede even the Sheriff in possession, excepting by an extent for the king; only with this provision:–

That if the Sheriff be in possession by warrant on judgment obtained by due course of law, and without fraud or deceit, and, bona fide, in possession before the debtor entered his name in the office, in such case the plaintiff to have a double dividend allotted to his debt; for it was the fault of the debtor to let execution come upon his goods before he sought for protection; but this not to be allowed upon judgment confessed.

If the Sheriff be in possession by fieri facias for debt immediately due to the king, the officer, however, shall quit his possession to the commissioners, and they shall see the king's debt fully satisfied before any division be made to the creditors.

The officers in this case to take no fee from the bankrupt, nor to use any indecent or uncivil behaviour to the family (which is a most notorious abuse now permitted to the sheriff's officers), whose fees I have known, on small executions, on pretence of civility, amount to as much as the debt, and yet behave themselves with unsufferable insolence all the while.

This officer being in possession, the goods may be removed, or not removed; the shop shut up or not shut up; as the bankrupt upon his reasons given to the commissioners may desire.

The inventory being taken, the bankrupt shall have fourteen days' time, and more if desired, upon showing good reasons to the commissioners, to settle his books and draw up his accounts; and then shall deliver up all his books, together with a full and true account of his whole estate, real and personal, to which account he shall make oath, and afterwards to any particular of it, if the commissioners require.

After this account given in, the commissioners shall have power to examine upon oath all his servants, or any other person; and if it appears that he has concealed anything, in breach of his oath, to punish him, as is hereafter specified.

Upon a fair and just surrender of all his estate and effects, bona fide, according to the true intent and meaning of the act, the commissioners shall return to him in money, or such of his goods as he shall choose, at a value by a just appraisement, 5 pounds per cent. of all the estate he surrendered, together with a full and free discharge from all his creditors.

The remainder of the estate of the debtor to be fairly and equally divided among the creditors, who are to apply themselves to the commissioners. The commissioners to make a necessary inquiry into the nature and circumstances of the debts demanded, that no pretended debt be claimed for the private account of the debtor; in order to which inquiry they shall administer the following oath to the creditor, for the proof of the debt.

I, A. B., do solemnly swear and attest that the account hereto annexed is true and right, and every article therein rightly and truly stated and charged in the names of the persons to whom they belong; and that there is no person or name named, concealed, or altered in the said account by me, or by my knowledge, order, or consent. And that the said does really and bona fide owe and stand indebted to me for my own proper account the full sum of mentioned in the said account, and that for a fair and just value made good to him, as by the said account expressed; and also that I have not made or known of any private contract, promise, or agreement between him the said (or any body for him) and me, or any person whatsoever.

So help me God.

Upon this oath, and no circumstances to render the person suspected, the creditor shall have an unquestioned right to his dividend, which shall be made without the delays and charges that attend the commissions of bankrupts. For,

1. The goods of the debtor shall upon the first meeting of the creditors be either sold in parcels, as

they shall agree, or divided among them in due proportion to their debts.

2. What debts are standing out, the debtors shall receive summonses from the commissioners, to pay by a certain time limited; and in the meantime the secretary is to transmit accounts to the persons owing it, appointing them a reasonable time to consent or disprove the account.

And every six months a just dividend shall be made among the creditors of the money received; and so, if the effects lie abroad, authentic procurations shall be signed by the bankrupt to the commissioners, who thereupon correspond with the persons abroad, in whose hands such effects are, who are to remit the same as the commissioners order; the dividend to be made, as before, every six months, or oftener, if the court see cause.

If any man thinks the bankrupt has so much favour by these articles, that those who can dispense with an oath have an opportunity to cheat their creditors, and that hereby too much encouragement is given to men to turn bankrupt; let them consider the easiness of the discovery, the difficulty of a concealment, and the penalty on the offender.

1. I would have a reward of 30 per cent. be provided to be paid to any person who should make discovery of any part of the bankrupt's estate concealed by him, which would make discoveries easy and frequent.

2. Any person who should claim any debt among the creditors, for the account of the bankrupt, or his wife or children, or with design to relieve them out of it, other or more than is, bona fide, due to him for value received, and to be made out; or any person who shall receive in trust, or by deed of gift, any part of the goods or other estate of the bankrupt, with design to preserve them for the use of the said bankrupt, or his wife or children, or with design to conceal them from the creditors, shall forfeit for every such act 500 pounds, and have his name published as a cheat, and a person not fit to be credited by any man. This would make it very difficult for the bankrupt to conceal anything.

3. The bankrupt having given his name, and put the officer into possession, shall not remove out of the house any of his books; but during the fourteen days' time which he shall have to settle the accounts shall every night deliver the books into the hands of the officer; and the commissioners shall have liberty, if they please, to take the books the first day, and cause duplicates to be made, and then to give them back to the bankrupt to settle the accounts.

4. If it shall appear that the bankrupt has given in a false account, has concealed any part of his goods or debts, in breach of his oath, he shall be set in the pillory at his own door, and be imprisoned during life without bail.

5. To prevent the bankrupt concealing any debts abroad, it should be enacted that the name of the bankrupt being entered at the office, where every man might search gratis, should be publication enough; and that after such entry, no discharge from the bankrupt should be allowed in account to any man, but whoever would adventure to pay any money to the said bankrupt or his order should be still debtor to the estate, and pay it again to the commissioners.

And whereas wiser heads than mine must be employed to compose this law, if ever it be made, they will have time to consider of more ways to secure the estate for the creditors, and, if possible, to tie the hands of the bankrupt yet faster.

This law, if ever such a happiness should arise to this kingdom, would be a present remedy for a multitude of evils which now we feel, and which are a sensible detriment to the trade of this nation.

1. With submission, I question not but it would prevent a great number of bankrupts, which now fall by divers causes. For,

(1.) It would effectually remove all crafty designed breakings, by which many honest men are ruined. And

(2.) Of course 'twould prevent the fall of those tradesmen who are forced to break by the knavery of such.

2. It would effectually suppress all those sanctuaries and refuges of thieves, the Mint, Friars, Savoy, Rules, and the like; and that these two ways:–

(1.) Honest men would have no need of it, here being a more safe, easy, and more honourable way to get out of trouble.

(2.) Knaves should have no protection from those places, and the Act be fortified against those places by the following clauses, which I have on purpose reserved to this head.

Since the provision this court of inquiries makes for the ease and deliverance of every debtor who is honest is so considerable, 'tis most certain that no man but he who has a design to cheat his creditors will refuse to accept of the favour; and therefore it should be enacted,

That if any man who is a tradesman or merchant shall break or fail, or shut up shop, or leave off trade, and shall not either pay or secure to his creditors their full and whole debts, twenty shillings in the pound, without abatement or deduction; or shall convey away their books or goods, in order to bring their creditors to any composition; or shall not apply to this office as aforesaid, shall be guilty of felony, and upon conviction of the same shall suffer as a felon, without benefit of clergy.

And if any such person shall take sanctuary either in the Mint, Friars, or other pretended privilege place, or shall convey thither any of their goods as aforesaid, to secure them from their creditors, upon complaint thereof made to any of His Majesty's Justices of the Peace, they shall immediately grant warrants to the constable, to search for the said persons and goods, who shall be aided and assisted by the trained bands, if need be, without any charge to the creditors, to search for, and discover the said persons and goods; and whoever were aiding in the carrying in the said goods, or whoever knowingly received either the goods or the person, should be also guilty of felony.

For as the indigent debtor is a branch of the commonwealth which deserves its care, so the wilful bankrupt is one of the worst sort of thieves. And it seems a little unequal that a poor fellow who for mere want steals from his neighbour some trifle shall be sent out of the kingdom, and sometimes out of the world, while a sort of people who defy justice, and violently resist the law, shall be suffered to carry men's estates away before their faces, and no officers to be found who dare execute the law upon them.

Any man would be concerned to hear with what scandal and reproach foreigners do speak of the impotence of our constitution in this point; that in a civilised Government, as ours is, the strangest contempt of authority is shown that can be instanced in the world.

I may be a little the warmer on this head, on account that I have been a larger sufferer by such means than ordinary. But I appeal to all the world as to the equity of the case. What the difference is between having my house broken up in the night to be robbed, and a man coming in good credit, and with a proffer of ready money in the middle of the day, and buying 500 pounds of goods, and carrying them directly from my warehouse into the Mint, and the next day laugh at me, and bid me defiance; yet this I have seen done. I think 'tis the justest thing in the world that the last should be esteemed the greater thief, and deserves most to be hanged.

I have seen a creditor come with his wife and children, and beg of the debtor only to let him have part of his own goods again, which he had bought, knowing and designing to break. I have seen him with tears and entreaties petition for his own, or but some of it, and be taunted and sworn at, and denied by a saucy insolent bankrupt. That the poor man has been wholly ruined by the cheat. It is by the villainy of such many an honest man is undone, families starved and sent a begging, and yet no punishment prescribed by our laws for it.

By the aforesaid commission of inquiry all this might be most effectually prevented, an honest, indigent tradesman preserved, knavery detected and punished; Mints, Friars, and privilege-places suppressed, and without doubt a great number of insolencies avoided and prevented; of which many more particulars might be insisted upon, but I think these may be sufficient to lead anybody into the thought; and for the method, I leave it to the wise heads of the nation, who know better than I how to state the law to the circumstances of the crime.

OF ACADEMIES.

***

We have in England fewer of these than in any part of the world, at least where learning is in so much esteem. But to make amends, the two great seminaries we have are, without comparison, the greatest, I won't say the best, in the world; and though much might be said here concerning universities in general, and foreign academies in particular, I content myself with noting that part in which we seem defective. The French, who justly value themselves upon erecting the most celebrated academy of Europe, owe the lustre of it very much to the great encouragement the kings of France have given to it. And one of the members making a speech at his entrance tells you that it is not the least of the glories of their invincible monarch to have engrossed all the learning of the world in that sublime body.

The peculiar study of the academy of Paris has been to refine and correct their own language, which they have done to that happy degree that we see it now spoken in all the courts of Christendom, as the language allowed to be most universal.

I had the honour once to be a member of a small society, who seemed to offer at this noble design in England. But the greatness of the work, and the modesty of the gentlemen concerned, prevailed with them to desist an enterprise which appeared too great for private hands to undertake. We want, indeed, a

Richelieu to commence such a work. For I am persuaded were there such a genius in our kingdom to lead the way, there would not want capacities who could carry on the work to a glory equal to all that has gone before them. The English tongue is a subject not at all less worthy the labour of such a society than the French, and capable of a much greater perfection. The learned among the French will own that the comprehensiveness of expression is a glory in which the English tongue not only equals but excels its neighbours; Rapin, St. Evremont, and the most eminent French authors have acknowledged it. And my lord Roscommon, who is allowed to be a good judge of English, because he wrote it as exactly as any ever did, expresses what I mean in these lines:-

> "For who did ever in French authors see
> The comprehensive English energy?
> The weighty bullion of one sterling line,
> Drawn to French wire would through whole pages shine."

"And if our neighbours will yield us, as their greatest critic has done, the preference for sublimity and nobleness of style, we will willingly quit all pretensions to their insignificant gaiety."

It is great pity that a subject so noble should not have some as noble to attempt it. And for a method, what greater can be set before us than the academy of Paris? Which, to give the French their due, stands foremost among all the great attempts in the learned part of the world.

The present King of England, of whom we have seen the whole world writing panegyrics and encomiums, and whom his enemies, when their interest does not silence them, are apt to say more of than ourselves; as in the war he has given surprising instances of a greatness of spirit more than common: so in peace, I daresay, with submission, he shall never have an opportunity to illustrate his memory more than by such a foundation. By which he shall have opportunity to darken the glory of the French king in peace, as he has by his daring attempts in the war.

Nothing but pride loves to be flattered, and that only as it is a vice which blinds us to our own imperfections. I think princes as particularly unhappy in having their good actions magnified as their evil actions covered. But King William, who has already won praise by the steps of dangerous virtue, seems reserved for some actions which are above the touch of flattery, whose praise is in themselves.

And such would this be. And because I am speaking of a work which seems to be proper only for the hand of the king himself, I shall not presume to carry on this chapter to the model, as I have done in other subjects. Only thus far:

That a society be erected by the king himself, if his Majesty thought fit, and composed of none but persons of the first figure in learning; and it were to be wished our gentry were so much lovers of learning that birth might always be joined with capacity.

The work of this society should be to encourage polite learning, to polish and refine the English tongue, and advance the so much neglected faculty of correct language, to establish purity and propriety of style, and to purge it from all the irregular additions that ignorance and affectation have introduced; and all those innovations in speech, if I may call them such, which some dogmatic writers have the confidence to foster upon their native language, as if their authority were sufficient to make their own fancy legitimate.

By such a society I daresay the true glory of our English style would appear; and among all the learned part of the world be esteemed, as it really is, the noblest and most comprehensive of all the vulgar languages in the world.

Into this society should be admitted none but persons eminent for learning, and yet none, or but very few, whose business or trade was learning. For I may be allowed, I suppose, to say we have seen many great scholars mere learned men, and graduates in the last degree of study, whose English has been far from polite, full of stiffness and affectation, hard words, and long unusual coupling of syllables and sentences, which sound harsh and untuneable to the ear, and shock the reader both in expression and understanding.

In short, there should be room in this society for neither clergyman, physician, nor lawyer. Not that I would put an affront upon the learning of any of those honourable employments, much less upon their persons. But if I do think that their several professions do naturally and severally prescribe habits of speech to them peculiar to their practice, and prejudicial to the study I speak of, I believe I do them no wrong. Nor do I deny but there may be, and now are, among some of all those professions men of style and language, great masters of English, whom few men will undertake to correct; and where such do at any time appear, their extraordinary merit should find them a place in this society; but it should be rare, and upon very extraordinary occasions that such be admitted.

I would therefore have this society wholly composed of gentlemen; whereof twelve to be of the nobility, if possible, and twelve private gentlemen, and a class of twelve to be left open for mere merit, let it be found in who or what sort it would, which should lie as the crown of their study, who have done something eminent to deserve it. The voice of this society should be sufficient authority for the usage of words, and sufficient also to expose the innovations of other mens fancies; they should preside with a sort of judicature over the learning of the age, and have liberty to correct and censure the exorbitance of writers, especially of translators. The reputation of this society would be enough to make them the allowed judges of style and language, and no author would have the impudence to coin without their authority. Custom, which is now our best authority for words, would always have its original here, and not be allowed without it. There should be no more occasion to search for derivations and constructions, and 'twould be as criminal then to coin words as money.

The exercises of this society would be lectures on the English tongue, essays on the nature, original, usage, authorities, and differences of words, or the propriety, parity, and cadence of style, and of the politeness and manner in writing; reflections upon irregular usages, and corrections of erroneous customs in words; and, in short, everything that would appear necessary to the bringing our English tongue to a due perfection, and our gentlemen to a capacity of writing like themselves; to banish pride and pedantry, and silence the impudence and impertinence of young authors, whose ambition is to be known, though it be by their folly.

I ask leave here for a thought or two about that inundation custom has made upon our language and discourse by familiar swearing; and I place it here, because custom has so far prevailed in this foolish vice that a man's discourse is hardly agreeable without it; and some have taken upon them to say it is pity it should not be lawful, it is such a grace in a man's speech, and adds so much vigour to his language.

I desire to be understood right, and that by swearing I mean all those cursory oaths, curses, execrations, imprecations, asseverations, and by whatsoever other names they are distinguished, which are used in vehemence of discourse, in the mouths almost of all men more or less, of what sort soever.

I am not about to argue anything of their being sinful and unlawful, as forbid by divine rules; let the parson alone to tell you that, who has, no question, said as much to as little purpose in this case as in any other. But I am of the opinion that there is nothing so impertinent, so insignificant, so senseless, and foolish as our vulgar way of discourse when mixed with oaths and curses, and I would only recommend a little consideration to our gentlemen, who have sense and wit enough, and would be ashamed to speak nonsense in other things, but value themselves upon their parts, I would but ask them to put into writing the commonplaces of their discourse, and read them over again, and examine the English, the cadence, the grammar of them; then let then turn them into Latin, or translate them into any other language, and but see what a jargon and confusion of speech they make together.

Swearing, that lewdness of the tongue, that scum and excrement of the mouth, is of all vices the most foolish and senseless. It makes a man's conversation unpleasant, his discourse fruitless, and his language nonsense.

It makes conversation unpleasant, at least to those who do not use the same foolish way of discourse, and, indeed, is an affront to all the company who swear not as he does; for if I swear and curse in company I either presume all the company likes it or affront them who do not.

Then it is fruitless; for no man is believed a jot the more for all the asseverations, damnings, and swearings he makes. Those who are used to it themselves do not believe a man the more because they know they are so customary that they signify little to bind a man's intention, and they who practise them not have so mean an opinion of those that do as makes them think they deserve no belief.

Then, they are the spoilers and destroyers of a man's discourse, and turn it into perfect nonsense; and to make it out I must descend a little to particulars, and desire the reader a little to foul his mouth with the brutish, sordid, senseless expressions which some gentlemen call polite English, and speaking with a grace.

Some part of them indeed, though they are foolish enough, as effects of a mad, inconsiderate rage, are yet English; as when a man swears he will do this or, that, and it may be adds, "God damn him he will;" that is, "God damn him if he don't." This, though it be horrid in another sense, yet may be read in writing, and is English: but what language is this?

"Jack, God damn me, Jack, how dost do? How hast thou done this long time, by God?" And then they kiss; and the other, as lewd as himself, goes on:–

"Dear Tom, I am glad to see thee with all my heart, let me die. Come, let us go take a bottle, we must not part so; pr'ythee let's go and be drunk by God."

This is some of our new florid language, and the graces and delicacies of style, which if it were put into Latin, I would fain know which is the principal verb.

But for a little further remembrance of this impertinence, go among the gamesters, and there nothing is more frequent than, "God damn the dice," or "God damn the bowls."

Among the sportsmen it is, "God damn the hounds," when they are at a fault; or, "God damn the horse," if he baulks a leap. They call men "sons of –," and "dogs," and innumerable instances may be given of the like gallantry of language, grown now so much a custom.

It is true, custom is allowed to be our best authority for words, and it is fit it should be so; but reason must be the judge of sense in language, and custom can never prevail over it. Words, indeed, like ceremonies in religion, may be submitted to the magistrate; but sense, like the essentials, is positive, unalterable, and cannot be submitted to any jurisdiction; it is a law to itself; it is ever the same; even an Act of Parliament cannot alter it.

Words, and even usages in style, may be altered by custom, and proprieties in speech differ according to the several dialects of the country, and according to the different manner in which several languages do severally express themselves.

But there is a direct signification of words, or a cadence in expression, which we call speaking sense; this, like truth, is sullen and the same, ever was and will be so, in what manner, and in what language soever it is expressed. Words without it are only noise, which any brute can make as well as we, and birds much better; for words without sense make but dull music. Thus a man may speak in words, but perfectly unintelligible as to meaning; he may talk a great deal, but say nothing. But it is the proper position of words, adapted to their significations, which makes them intelligible, and conveys the meaning of the speaker to the understanding of the hearer; the contrary to which we call nonsense; and there is a superfluous crowding in of insignificant words, more than are needful to express the thing intended, and this is impertinence; and that again, carried to an extreme, is ridiculous.

Thus when our discourse is interlined with needless oaths, curses, and long parentheses of imprecations, and with some of very indirect signification, they become very impertinent; and these being run to the extravagant degree instanced in before, become perfectly ridiculous and nonsense, and without forming it into an argument, it appears to be nonsense by the contradictoriness; and it appears impertinent by the insignificancy of the expression.

After all, how little it becomes a gentleman to debauch his mouth with foul language, I refer to themselves in a few particulars.

This vicious custom has prevailed upon good manners too far; but yet there are some degrees to which it has not yet arrived.

As, first, the worst slaves to this folly will neither teach it to nor approve of it in their children. Some of the most careless will indeed negatively teach it by not reproving them for it; but sure no man ever ordered his children to be taught to curse or swear.

2. The grace of swearing has not obtained to be a mode yet among the women: "God damn ye" does not fit well upon a female tongue; it seems to be a masculine vice, which the women are not arrived to yet; and I would only desire those gentlemen who practice it themselves to hear a woman swear: it has no music at all there, I am sure; and just as little does it become any gentleman, if he would suffer himself to be judged by all the laws of sense or good manners in the world.

It is a senseless, foolish, ridiculous practice; it is a mean to no manner of end; it is words spoken which signify nothing; it is folly acted for the sake of folly, which is a thing even the devil himself don't practice. The devil does evil, we say, but it is for some design, either to seduce others, or, as some divines say, from a principle of enmity to his Maker. Men steal for gain, and murder to gratify their avarice or revenge; whoredoms and ravishments, adulteries and sodomy, are committed to please a vicious appetite, and have always alluring objects; and generally all vices have some previous cause, and some visible tendency. But this, of all vicious practices, seems the most nonsensical and ridiculous; there is neither pleasure nor profit, no design pursued, no lust gratified, but is a mere frenzy of the tongue, a vomit of the brain, which works by putting a contrary upon the course of nature.

Again, other vices men find some reason or other to give for, or excuses to palliate. Men plead want to extenuate theft, and strong provocations to excuse murders, and many a lame excuse they will bring for whoring; but this sordid habit even those that practise it will own to be a crime, and make no excuse for it; and the most I could ever hear a man say for it was that he could not help it.

Besides, as it is an inexcusable impertinence, so it is a breach upon good manners and conversation, for a man to impose the clamour of his oaths upon the company he converses with; if there be any one person in the company that does not approve the way, it is an imposing upon him with a freedom beyond civility.

To suppress this, laws, Acts of Parliament, and proclamations are baubles and banters, the laughter of the lewd party, and never had, as I could perceive, any influence upon the practice; nor are any of our magistrates fond or forward of putting them in execution.

It must be example, not penalties, must sink this crime; and if the gentlemen of England would once drop it as a mode, the vice is so foolish and ridiculous in itself, it would soon grow odious and out of fashion.

This work such an academy might begin, and I believe nothing would so soon explode the practice as the public discouragement of it by such a society; where all our customs and habits, both in speech and behaviour, should receive an authority. All the disputes about precedency of wit, with the manners, customs, and usages of the theatre, would be decided here; plays should pass here before they were acted, and the critics might give their censures and damn at their pleasure; nothing would ever die which once received life at this original. The two theatres might end their jangle, and dispute for priority no more; wit and real worth should decide the controversy, and here should be the infallible judge.

The strife would then be only to do well,
And he alone be crowned who did excel.
Ye call them Whigs, who from the church withdrew,
But now we have our stage dissenters too,
Who scruple ceremonies of pit and box,
And very few are sound and orthodox,
But love disorder so, and are so nice,
They hate conformity, though 'tis in vice.
Some are for patent hierarchy; and some,
Like the old Gauls, seek out for elbow room;
Their arbitrary governors disown,
And build a conventicle stage of their own.
Fanatic beaux make up the gaudy show,

And wit alone appears incognito.
Wit and religion suffer equal fate;
Neglect of both attends the warm debate.
For while the parties strive and countermine,
Wit will as well as piety decline.

Next to this, which I esteem as the most noble and most useful proposal in this book, I proceed to academies for military studies, and because I design rather to express my meaning than make a large book, I bring them all into one chapter.

I allow the war is the best academy in the world, where men study by necessity and practice by force, and both to some purpose, with duty in the action, and a reward in the end; and it is evident to any man who knows the world, or has made any observations on things, what an improvement the English nation has made during this seven years' war.

But should you ask how clear it first cost, and what a condition England was in for a war at first on this account – how almost all our engineers and great officers were foreigners, it may put us in mind how necessary it is to have our people so practised in the arts of war that they may not be novices when they come to the experiment.

I have heard some who were no great friends to the Government take advantage to reflect upon the king, in the beginning of his wars in Ireland, that he did not care to trust the English, but all his great officers, his generals, and engineers were foreigners. And though the case was so plain as to need no answer, and the persons such as deserved none, yet this must be observed, though it was very strange: that when the present king took possession of this kingdom, and, seeing himself entering upon the bloodiest war this age has known, began to regulate his army, he found but very few among the whole martial part of the nation fit to make use of for general officers, and was forced to employ strangers, and make them Englishmen (as the Counts Schomberg, Ginkel, Solms, Ruvigny, and others); and yet it is to be observed also that all the encouragement imaginable was given to the English gentlemen to qualify themselves, by giving no less than sixteen regiments to gentlemen of good families who had never been in any service and knew but very little how to command them. Of these, several are now in the army, and have the rewards suitable to their merit, being major-generals, brigadiers, and the like.

If, then, a long peace had so reduced us to a degree of ignorance that might have been dangerous to us, had we not a king who is always followed by the greatest masters in the world, who knows what peace and different governors may bring us to again?

The manner of making war differs perhaps as much as anything in the world; and if we look no further back than our civil wars, it is plain a general then would hardly be fit to be a colonel now, saving his capacity of improvement. The defensive art always follows the offensive; and though the latter has extremely got the start of the former in this age, yet the other is mightily improving also.

We saw in England a bloody civil war, where, according to the old temper of the English, fighting was the business. To have an army lying in such a post as not to be able to come at them was a thing never heard of in that war; even the weakest party would always come out and fight (Dunbar fight, for instance); and they that were beaten today would fight again tomorrow, and seek one another out with such eagerness, as if they had been in haste to have their brains knocked out. Encampments, intrenchments, batteries, counter-marchings, fortifying of camps, and cannonadings were strange and almost unknown things; and whole campaigns were passed over, and hardly any tents made use of. Battles, surprises, storming of towns, skirmishes, sieges, ambuscades, and beating up quarters was the news of every day. Now it is frequent to have armies of fifty thousand men of a side stand at bay within view of one another, and spend a whole campaign in dodging (or, as it is genteelly called, observing) one another, and then march off into winter quarters. The difference is in the maxims of war, which now differ as much from what they were formerly as long perukes do from piqued beards, or as the habits of the people do now from what they then were. The present maxims of the war are:

"Never fight without a manifest advantage."

"And always encamp so as not to be forced to it."

And if two opposite generals nicely observe both these rules, it is impossible they should ever come to fight.

I grant that this way of making war spends generally more money and less blood than former wars did; but then it spins wars out to a greater length; and I almost question whether, if this had been the way of fighting of old, our civil war had not lasted till this day. Their maxim was:

"Wherever you meet your enemy, fight him."

But the case is quite different now; and I think it is plain in the present war that it is not he who has the longest sword, so much as he who has the longest purse, will hold the war out best. Europe is all engaged in the war, and the men will never be exhausted while either party can find money; but he who finds himself poorest must give out first; and this is evident in the French king, who now inclines to peace, and owns it, while at the same time his armies are numerous and whole. But the sinews fail; he finds his exchequer fail, his kingdom drained, and money hard to come at: not that I believe half the reports we have had of the misery and poverty of the French are true; but it is manifest the King of France finds, whatever his armies may do, his money won't hold out so long as the Confederates, and therefore he uses all the means possible to procure a peace, while he may do it with the most advantage.

There is no question but the French may hold the war out several years longer; but their king is too wise to let things run to extremity. He will rather condescend to peace upon hard terms now than stay longer, if he finds himself in danger to be forced to worse.

This being the only digression I design to be guilty of, I hope I shall be excused it.

The sum of all is this: that, since it is so necessary to be in a condition for war in a time of peace, our people should be inured to it. It is strange that everything should be ready but the soldier: ships are ready, and our trade keeps the seamen always taught, and breeds up more; but soldiers, horsemen, engineers, gunners, and the like must be bred and taught; men are not born with muskets on their shoulders, nor fortifications in their heads; it is not natural to shoot bombs and undermine towns: for which purpose I propose a

ROYAL ACADEMY FOR MILITARY EXERCISES.

The founder the king himself; the charge to be paid by the public, and settled by a revenue from the Crown, to be paid yearly.

I propose this to consist of four parts:

1. A college for breeding up of artists in the useful practice of all military exercises; the scholars to be taken in young, and be maintained, and afterwards under the king's care for preferment, as their merit and His Majesty's favour shall recommend them; from whence His Majesty would at all times be furnished

with able engineers, gunners, fire-masters. bombardiers, miners, and the like.

The second college for voluntary students in the same exercises; who should all upon certain limited conditions be entertained, and have all the advantages of the lectures, experiments, and learning of the college, and be also capable of several titles, profits, and settlements in the said college, answerable to the Fellows in the Universities.

The third college for temporary study, into which any person who is a gentleman and an Englishman, entering his name and conforming to the orders of the house, shall be entertained like a gentleman for one whole year gratis, and taught by masters appointed out of the second college.

The fourth college, of schools only, where all persons whatsoever for a small allowance shall be taught and entered in all the particular exercises they desire; and this to be supplied by the proficients of the first college.

I could lay out the dimensions and necessary incidents of all this work, but since the method of such a foundation is easy and regular from the model of other colleges, I shall only state the economy of the house.

The building must be very large, and should rather be stately and magnificent in figure than gay and costly in ornament: and I think such a house as Chelsea College, only about four times as big, would answer it; and yet, I believe, might be finished for as little charge as has been laid out in that palace-like hospital.

The first college should consist of one general, five colonels, twenty captains.

Being such as graduates by preferment, at first named by the founder; and after the first settlement to be chosen out of the first or second colleges; with apartments in the college, and salaries.

	Pounds per ann.
The general	300
The colonels	100
The captains	60

2,000 scholars, among whom shall be the following degrees:

	Pounds per ann.
Governors	100 allowed 10
Directors	200 5
Exempts	200 5
Proficients	500
Juniors	1,000

The general to be named by the founder, out of the colonels; the colonels to be named by the general, out of the captains; the captains out of the governors; the governors from the directors; and the directors from the exempts; and so on.

The juniors to be divided into ten schools; the schools to be thus governed: every school has
100 juniors, in 10 classes.

Every class to have 2 directors.	
100 classes of juniors is	1,000
Each class 2 directors	200
	=====
	1,200

The proficients to be divided into five schools:

Every school to have ten classes of 10 each.	
Every class 2 governors.	
50 classes of proficients is	500
Each class 2 governors is	100
	===
	600

The exempts to be supernumerary, having a small allowance, and maintained in the college till preferment offer.

The second college to consist of voluntary students, to be taken in, after a certain degree of learning, from among the proficients of the first, or from any other schools, after such and such limitations of learning; who study at their own charge, being allowed certain privileges; as–

Chambers rent-free on condition of residence.

Commons gratis, for certain fixed terms.

Preferment, on condition of a term of years' residence.

Use of libraries, instruments, and lectures of the college.

This college should have the following preferments, with salaries

	Pounds per ann.
A governor	200
A president	100
50 college-majors	50
200 proficients	10
500 voluntary students, without allowance	

The third and fourth colleges, consisting only of schools for temporary study, may be thus:

The third - being for gentlemen to learn the necessary arts and exercises to qualify them for the service of their country, and entertaining them one whole year at the public charge - may be supposed to have always one thousand persons on its hands, and cannot have less than 100 teachers, whom I would thus order:

> Every teacher shall continue at least one year, but by allowance two years at most; shall have 20 pounds per annum extraordinary allowance; shall be bound to give their constant attendance; and shall have always five college-majors of the second college to supervise them, who shall command a month, and then be succeeded by five others, and,

so on – 10 pounds per annum extraordinary to be paid them for their attendance.

The gentlemen who practise to be put to no manner of charge, but to be obliged strictly to the following articles:

1. To constant residence, not to lie out of the house without leave of the college-major.

2. To perform all the college exercises, as appointed by the masters, without dispute.

3. To submit to the orders of the house.

To quarrel or give ill-language should be a crime to be punished by way of fine only, the college-major to be judge, and the offender be put into custody till he ask pardon of the person wronged; by which means every gentleman who has been affronted has sufficient satisfaction.

But to strike challenge, draw, or fight, should be more severely punished; the offender to be declared no gentleman, his name posted up at the college-gate, his person expelled the house, and to be pumped as a rake if ever he is taken within the college-walls.

The teachers of this college to be chosen, one half out of the exempts of the first college, and the other out of the proficients of the second.

The fourth college, being only of schools, will be neither chargeable nor troublesome, but may consist of as many as shall offer themselves to be taught, and supplied with teachers from the other schools.

The proposal, being of so large an extent, must have a proportionable settlement for its maintenance; and the benefit being to the whole kingdom, the charge will naturally lie upon the public, and cannot well be less, considering the number of persons to be maintained, than as follows.

FIRST COLLEGE.

	Pounds per ann.
The general	300
5 colonels at 100 pounds per ann. each	500
20 captains at 60	1,200
100 governors at 10	1,000
200 directors at 5	1,000
200 exempts at 5	1,000
2,000 heads for subsistence, at 20 pounds per head per ann., including provision, and all the officers' salaries in the house, as butlers, cooks, purveyors, nurses, maids, laundresses, stewards, clerks, servants, chaplains, porters, and attendants, which are numerous.	40,000

SECOND COLLEGE.

A governor	200
A president	100
50 college-majors at 50 pounds per ann. each	2,500
200 proficients at 10	2,000
Commons for 500 students during times of exercises at 5 pounds per ann. each	2,500

200 proficients' subsistence, reckoning as above	4,000
THIRD COLLEGE.	
The gentlemen here are maintained as gentlemen, and are to have good tables, who shall therefore have an allowance at the rate of 25 pounds per head, all officers to be maintained out of it; which is	25,000
100 teachers, salary and subsistence ditto	4,500
50 college-majors at 10 pounds per ann. is	500
	======
Annual charge	86,300
The building to cost	50,000
Furniture, beds, tables, chairs, linen, &c	10,000
Books, instruments, and utensils for experiments	2,000
	======
So the immediate charge would be	62,000
The annual charge	86,300
To which add the charges of exercises and experiments	90,000

The king's magazines to furnish them with 500 barrels of gunpowder per annum for the public uses of exercises and experiments.

In the first of these colleges should remain the governing part, and all the preferments to be made from thence, to be supplied in course from the other; the general of the first to give orders to the other, and be subject only to the founder.

The government should be all military, with a constitution for the same regulated for that purpose, and a council to hear and determine the differences and trespasses by the college laws.

The public exercises likewise military, and all the schools be disciplined under proper officers, who are so in turn or by order of the general, and continue but for the day.

The several classes to perform several studies, and but one study to a distinct class, and the persons, as they remove from one study to another, to change their classes, but so as that in the general exercises all the scholars may be qualified to act all the several parts as they may be ordered.

The proper studies of this college should be the following:

Geometry.	Bombarding.
Astronomy.	Gunnery.
History.	Fortification.
Navigation.	Encamping.
Decimal arithmetic.	Intrenching.
Trigonometry.	Approaching.
Dialing.	Attacking.
Gauging.	Delineation.
Mining.	Architecture.
Fireworking.	Surveying.

And all arts or sciences appendices to such as these, with exercises for the body, to which all should be obliged, as their genius and capacities led them, as:

1. Swimming; which no soldier, and, indeed, no man whatever, ought to be without.
2. Handling all sorts of firearms.
3. Marching and counter-marching in form.
4. Fencing and the long-staff.
5. Riding and managing, or horsemanship.
6. Running, leaping, and wrestling.

And herewith should also be preserved and carefully taught all the customs, usages, terms of war, and terms of art used in sieges, marches of armies and encampments, that so a gentleman taught in this college should be no novice when he comes into the king's armies, though he has seen no service abroad. I remember the story of an English gentleman, an officer at the siege of Limerick, in Ireland, who, though he was brave enough upon action, yet for the only matter of being ignorant in the terms of art, and knowing not how to talk camp language, was exposed to be laughed at by the whole army for mistaking the opening of the trenches, which he thought had been a mine against the town.

The experiments of these colleges would be as well worth publishing as the acts of the Royal Society. To which purpose the house must be built where they may have ground to cast bombs, to raise regular works, as batteries, bastions, half-moons, redoubts, horn-works, forts, and the like; with the convenience of water to draw round such works, to exercise the engineers in all the necessary experiments of draining and mining under ditches. There must be room to fire great shot at a distance, to cannonade a camp, to throw all sorts of fireworks and machines that are, or shall be, invented; to open trenches, form camps,

Their public exercises will be also very diverting, and more worth while for any gentleman to see than the sights or shows which our people in England are so fond of.

I believe as a constitution might be formed from these generals, this would be the greatest, the gallantest and the most useful foundation in the world. The English gentry would be the best qualified, and consequently best accepted abroad, and most useful at home of any people in the world; and His Majesty should never more be exposed to the necessity of employing foreigners in the posts of trust and service in his armies.

And that the whole kingdom might in some degree be better qualified for service, I think the following project would be very useful:

When our military weapon was the longbow, at which our English nation in some measure excelled the whole world, the meanest countryman was a good archer; and that which qualified them so much for service in the war was their diversion in times of peace, which also had this good effect – that when an army was to be raised they needed no disciplining:

and for the encouragement of the people to an exercise so publicly profitable an Act of Parliament was made to oblige every parish to maintain butts for the youth in the country to shoot at.

Since our way of fighting is now altered, and this destructive engine the musket is the proper arms for the soldier, I could wish the diversion also of the English would change too, that our pleasures and profit might correspond. It is a great hindrance to this nation, especially where standing armies are a grievance, that if ever a war commence, men must have at least a year before they are thought fit to face an enemy, to instruct them how to handle their arms; and new-raised men are called raw soldiers. To help this - at least, in some, measure - I would propose that the public exercises of our youth should by some public encouragement (for penalties won't do it) be drawn off from the foolish boyish sports of cocking and cricketing, and from tippling, to shooting with a firelock (an exercise as pleasant as it is manly and generous) and swimming, which is a thing so many ways profitable, besides its being a great preservative of health, that methinks no man ought to be without it.

1. For shooting, the colleges I have mentioned above, having provided for the instructing the gentry at the king's charge, that the gentry, in return of a favour, should introduce it among the country people, which might easily be done thus:

If every country gentleman, according to his degree, would contribute to setup a prize to be shot for by the town he lives in or the neighbourhood, about once a year, or twice a year, or oftener, as they think fit; which prize not single only to him who shoots nearest, but according to the custom of shooting.

This would certainly set all the young men in England a-shooting, and make them marksmen; for they would be always practising, and making matches among themselves too, and the advantage would be found in a war; for, no doubt, if all the soldiers in a battalion took a true level at their enemy there would be much more execution done at a distance than there is; whereas it has been known how that a battalion of men has received the fire of another battalion, and not lost above thirty or forty men; and I suppose it will not easily be forgotten how, at the battle of Agrim, a battalion of the English army received the whole fire of an Irish regiment of Dragoons, but never knew to this day whether they had any bullets or no; and I need appeal no further than to any officer that served in the Irish war, what advantages the English armies made of the Irish being such wonderful marksmen.

Under this head of academies I might bring in a project for an

ACADEMY FOR WOMEN

I have often thought of it as one of the most barbarous customs in the world, considering us as a civilised and a Christian country, that we deny the advantages of learning to women. We reproach the sex every day with folly and impertinence, while I am confident, had they the advantages of education equal to us, they would be guilty of less than ourselves.

One would wonder indeed how it should happen that women are conversable at all, since they are only beholding to natural parts for all their knowledge. Their youth is spent to teach them to stitch and sew, or make baubles. They are taught to read indeed, and perhaps to write their names, or so, and that is the height of a woman's education. And I would but ask any who slight the sex for their understanding, What is a man (a gentleman, I mean) good for that is taught no more?

I need not give instances, or examine the character of a gentleman with a good estate, and of a good family, and with tolerable parts, and examine what figure he makes for want of education.

The soul is placed in the body like a rough diamond, and must be polished, or the lustre of it will never appear. And it is manifest that as the rational soul distinguishes us from brutes, so education carries on the distinction, and makes some less brutish than others. This is too evident to need any demonstration. But why, then, should women be denied the benefit of instruction? If knowledge and understanding had been useless additions to the sex, God Almighty would never have given them capacities, for He made nothing needless: besides, I would ask such what they can see in ignorance that they should think it a necessary ornament to a woman. Or, How much worse is a wise woman than a fool? or, What has the woman done to forfeit the privilege of being taught? Does she plague us with her pride and impertinence? Why did we not let her learn, that she might have had more wit? Shall we upbraid women with folly, when it is only the error of this inhuman custom that hindered them being made wiser?

The capacities of women are supposed to be greater and their senses quicker than those of the men; and what they might be capable of being bred to is plain from some instances of female wit which this age is not without, which upbraids us with injustice, and looks as if we denied women the advantages of education for fear they should vie with the men in their improvements.

To remove this objection, and that women might have at least a needful opportunity of education in all sorts of useful learning, I propose the draft of an academy for that purpose.

I know it is dangerous to make public appearances of the sex; they are not either to be confined or exposed: the first will disagree with their inclinations, and the last with their reputations; and therefore it is somewhat difficult; and I doubt a method proposed by an ingenious lady, in a little book called, "Advice to the Ladies," would be found impracticable. For, saving my respect to the sex, the levity which perhaps is a little peculiar to them (at least in their youth) will not bear the restraint; and I am satisfied nothing but the height of bigotry can keep up a nunnery. Women are extravagantly desirous of going to heaven, and will punish their pretty bodies to get thither; but nothing else will do it, and even in that case sometimes it falls out that nature will prevail.

When I talk therefore of an academy for women I mean both the model, the teaching, and the government different from what is proposed by that ingenious lady, for whose proposal I have a very great esteem, and also a great opinion of her wit; different, too, from all sorts of religious confinement, and, above all, from vows of celibacy.

Wherefore the academy I propose should differ but little from public schools, wherein such ladies as were willing to study should have all the advantages of learning suitable to their genius.

But since some severities of discipline more than ordinary would be absolutely necessary to preserve the reputation of the house, that persons of quality and fortune might not be afraid to venture their children thither, I shall venture to make a small scheme by way of essay.

The house I would have built in a form by itself, as well as in a place by itself.

The building should be of three plain fronts, without any jettings or bearing-work, that the eye might at a glance see from one coin to the other; the gardens walled in the same triangular figure, with a large moat, and but one entrance.

When thus every part of the situation was contrived as well as might be for discovery, and to render intriguing dangerous, I would have no guards, no eyes, no spies set over the ladies, but shall expect them to be tried by the principles of honour and strict virtue.

And if I am asked why, I must ask pardon of my own sex for giving this reason for it:

I am so much in charity with women, and so well acquainted with men, that it is my opinion there needs no other care to prevent intriguing than to keep the men effectually away. For though inclination, which we prettily call love, does sometimes move a little too visibly in the sex, and frailty often follows, yet I think verily custom, which we miscall modesty, has so far the ascendant over the sex that solicitation always goes before it.

"Custom with women, 'stead of virtue, rules;
It leads the wisest, and commands the fools;
For this alone, when inclinations reign,
Though virtue's fled, will acts of vice restrain.
Only by custom 'tis that virtue lives,
And love requires to be asked before it gives.
For that which we call modesty is pride:
They scorn to ask, and hate to be denied.
'Tis custom thus prevails upon their want;
They'll never beg what, asked, they easily grant.

And when the needless ceremony's over,
Themselves the weakness of the sex discover.
If, then, desires are strong, and nature free,
Keep from her men and opportunity.
Else 'twill be vain to curb her by restraint;
But keep the question off, you keep the saint."

In short, let a woman have never such a coming principle, she will let you ask before she complies – at least, if she be a woman of any honour.

Upon this ground I am persuaded such measures might be taken that the ladies might have all the freedom in the world within their own walls, and yet no intriguing, no indecencies, nor scandalous affairs happen; and in order to this, the following customs and laws should be observed in the colleges, of which I would propose one at least in every county in England, and about ten for the city of London.

After the regulation of the form of the building as before;

1. All the ladies who enter into the house should set their hands to the orders of the house, to signify their consent to submit to them.

2. As no woman should be received but who declared herself willing, and that it was the act of her choice to enter herself, so no person should be confined to continue there a moment longer than the same voluntary choice inclined her.

3. The charges of the house being to be paid by the ladies, every one that entered should have only

this incumbrance – that she should pay for the whole year, though her mind should change as to her continuance.

4. An Act of Parliament should make it felony, without clergy, for any man to enter by force or fraud into the house, or to solicit any woman, though it were to marry, while she was in the house. And this law would by no means be severe, because any woman who was willing to receive the addresses of a man might discharge herself of the house when she pleased; and, on the contrary, any woman who had occasion might discharge herself of the impertinent addresses of any person she had an aversion to by entering into the house.

In this house the persons who enter should be taught all sorts of breeding suitable to both their genius and their quality, and, in particular, music and dancing, which it would be cruelty to bar the sex of, because they are their darlings; but, besides this, they should be taught languages, as particularly French and Italian; and I would venture the injury of giving a woman more tongues than one.

They should, as a particular study, be taught all the graces of speech, and all the necessary air of conversation, which our common education is so defective in that I need not expose it. They should be brought to read books, and especially history, and so to read as to make them understand the world, and be able to know and judge of things when they hear of them.

To such whose genius would lead them to it I would deny no sort of learning: but the chief thing in general is to cultivate the understandings of the sex, that they may be capable of all sorts of conversation; that, their parts and judgments being improved, they may be as profitable in their conversation as they are pleasant.

Women, in my observation, have little or no difference in them but as they are, or are not, distinguished by education. Tempers indeed may in some degree influence them, but the main distinguishing part is their breeding.

The whole sex are generally quick and sharp; I believe I may be allowed to say generally so; for you rarely see them lumpish and heavy when they are children, as boys will often be. If a woman be well bred, and taught the proper management of her natural wit, she proves generally very sensible and retentive; and, without partiality, a woman of sense and manners is the finest and most delicate part of God's creation, the glory of her Maker, and the great instance of His singular regard to man (His darling creature), to whom He gave the best gift either God could bestow or man receive; and it is the most sordid piece of folly and ingratitude in the world to withhold from the sex the due lustre which the advantages of education gives to the natural beauty of their minds.

A woman well bred and well taught, furnished with the additional accomplishments of knowledge and behaviour, is a creature without comparison; her society is the emblem of sublimer enjoyments; her person is angelic, and her conversation heavenly; she is all softness and sweetness, peace, love, wit, and delight; she is every way suitable to the sublimest wish, and the man that has such a one to his portion has nothing to do but to rejoice in her, and be thankful.

On the other hand, suppose her to be the very same woman, and rob her of the benefit of education, and it follows thus:

If her temper be good, want of education makes her soft and easy.

Her wit, for want of teaching, makes her impertinent and talkative.

Her knowledge, for want of judgment and experience, makes her fanciful and whimsical.

If her temper be bad, want of breeding makes her worse, and she grows haughty, insolent, and loud.

If she be passionate, want of manners makes her termagant and a scold, which is much at one with lunatic.

If she be proud, want of discretion (which still is breeding) makes her conceited, fantastic, and ridiculous.

And from these she degenerates to be turbulent, clamorous, noisy, nasty, and "the devil."

Methinks mankind for their own sakes (since, say what we will of the women, we all think fit one time or other to be concerned with them) should take some care to breed them up to be suitable and serviceable, if they expected no such thing as delight from them. Bless us! what care do we take to breed up a good horse, and to break him well! And what a value do we put upon him when it is done! – and all because he should be fit for our use. And why not a woman? – since all her ornaments and beauty, without suitable behaviour, is a cheat in nature, like the false tradesman who puts the best of his goods uppermost, that the buyer may think the rest are of the same goodness.

Beauty of the body, which is the women's glory, seems to be now unequally bestowed, and nature (or, rather, Providence) to lie under some scandal about it, as if it was given a woman for a snare to men, and so make a kind of a she-devil of her: because, they say, exquisite beauty is rarely given with wit, more rarely with goodness of temper, and never at all with modesty. And some, pretending to justify the equity of such a distribution, will tell us it is the effect of the justice of Providence in dividing particular excellences among all His creatures, "Share and share alike, as it were," that all might for something or other be acceptable to one another, else some would be despised.

I think both these notions false; and yet the last, which has the show of respect to Providence, is the worst; for it supposes Providence to be indigent and empty, as if it had not wherewith to furnish all the creatures it had made, but was fain to be parsimonious in its gifts, and distribute them by piecemeal, for fear of being exhausted.

If I might venture my opinion against an almost universal notion, I would say most men mistake the proceedings of Providence in this case, and all the world at this day are mistaken in their practice about it. And, because the assertion is very bold, I desire to explain myself.

That Almighty First Cause which made us all is certainly the fountain of excellence, as it is of being, and by an invisible influence could have diffused equal qualities and perfections to all the creatures it has made, as the sun does its light, without the least ebb or diminution to Himself; and has given indeed to every individual sufficient to the figure His providence had designed him in the world.

I believe it might be defended if I should say that I do suppose God has given to all mankind equal gifts and capacities, in that He has given them all souls equally capable; and that the whole difference in mankind proceeds either from accidental difference in the make of their bodies, or from the foolish difference of education.

1. FROM ACCIDENTAL DIFFERENCE IN BODIES. – I would avoid discoursing here of the philosophical position of the soul in the body: but if it be true, as philosophers do affirm, that the understanding and memory is dilated or contracted according to the accidental dimensions of the organ

through which it is conveyed, then, though God has given a soul as capable to me as another, yet if I have any natural defect in those parts of the body by which the soul should act, I may have the same soul infused as another man, and yet he be a wise man and I a very fool. For example, if a child naturally have a defect in the organ of hearing, so that he could never distinguish any sound, that child shall never be able to speak or read, though it have a soul capable of all the accomplishments in the world. The brain is the centre of the soul's actings, where all the distinguishing faculties of it reside; and it is observable, a man who has a narrow contracted head, in which there is not room for the due and necessary operations of nature by the brain, is never a man of very great judgment; and that proverb, "A great head and little wit," is not meant by nature, but is a reproof upon sloth; as if one should, by way of wonder say, "Fie, fie, you that have a great head have but little wit; that's strange! that must certainly be your own fault." From this notion I do believe there is a great matter in the breed of men and women; not that wise men shall always get wise children: but I believe strong and healthy bodies have the wisest children; and sickly, weakly bodies affect the wits as well as the bodies of their children. We are easily persuaded to believe this in the breeds of horses, cocks, dogs, and other creatures; and I believe it is as visible in men.

But to come closer to the business; the great distinguishing difference which is seen in the world between men and women is in their education; and this is manifested by comparing it with the difference between one man or woman and another.

And herein it is that I take upon me to make such a bold assertion, that all the world are mistaken in their practice about women: for I cannot think that God Almighty ever made them so delicate, so glorious creatures, and furnished them with such charms, so agreeable and so delightful to mankind, with souls capable of the same accomplishments with men, and all to be only stewards of our houses, cooks, and slaves.

Not that I am for exalting the female government in the least: but, in short, I would have men take women for companions, and educate them to be fit for it. A woman of sense and breeding will scorn as much to encroach upon the prerogative of the man as a man of sense will scorn to oppress the weakness of the woman. But if the women's souls were refined and improved by teaching, that word would be lost; to say, "the weakness of the sex," as to judgment, would be nonsense; for ignorance and folly would be no more to be found among women than men. I remember a passage which I heard from a very fine woman; she had wit and capacity enough, an extraordinary shape and face, and a great fortune, but had been cloistered up all her time, and, for fear of being stolen, had not had the liberty of being taught the common necessary knowledge of women's affairs; and when she came to converse in the world her natural wit made her so sensible of the want of education that she gave this short reflection on herself:

"I am ashamed to talk with my very maids," says she, "for I don't know when they do right or wrong: I had more need go to school than be married."

I need not enlarge on the loss the defect of education is to the sex, nor argue the benefit of the contrary practice; it is a thing will be more easily granted than remedied: this chapter is but an essay at the thing, and I refer the practice to those happy days, if ever they shall be, when men shall be wise enough to mend it.

OF A COURT MERCHANT.

***

I ask pardon of the learned gentlemen of the long robe if I do them any wrong in this chapter, having no design to affront them when I say that in matters of debate among merchants, when they come to be argued by lawyers at the bar, they are strangely handled. I myself have heard very famous lawyers make sorry work of a cause between the merchant and his factor; and when they come to argue about exchanges, discounts, protests, demurrages, charter-parties, freights, port-charges, assurances, barratries, bottomries, accounts current, accounts in commission, and accounts in company, and the like, the solicitor has not been able to draw a brief, nor the counsel to understand it. Never was young parson more put to it to make out his text when he is got into the pulpit without his notes than I have seen a counsel at the bar when he would make out a cause between two merchants. And I remember a pretty history of a particular case, by way of instance, when two merchants, contending about a long factorage account, that had all the niceties of merchandising in it, and labouring on both sides to instruct their counsel, and to put them in when they were out, at last they found them make such ridiculous stuff of it that they both threw up the cause and agreed to a reference, which reference in one week, without any charge, ended all the dispute, which they had spent a great deal of money in before to no purpose.

Nay, the very judges themselves (no reflection upon their learning) have been very much at a loss in giving instructions to a jury, and juries much more to understand them; for, when all is done, juries, which are not always, nor often indeed, of the wisest men, are, to be sure, in umpires in causes so nice that the very lawyer and judge can hardly understand them.

The affairs of merchants are accompanied with such variety of circumstances, such new and unusual contingencies, which change and differ in every age, with a multitude of niceties and punctilios (and those, again, altering as the customs and usages of countries and states do alter), that it has been found impracticable to make any laws that could extend to all cases. And our law itself does tacitly acknowledge its own imperfection in this case, by allowing the custom of merchants to pass as a kind of law in cases of difficulty.

Wherefore it seems to me a most natural proceeding that such affairs should be heard before, and judged by, such as by known experience and long practice in the customs and usages of foreign negotiation are of course the most capable to determine the same.

Besides the reasonableness of the argument there are some cases in our laws in which it is impossible for a plaintiff to make out his case, or a defendant to make out his plea; as, in particular, when his proofs are beyond seas (for no protests, certifications, or procurations are allowed in our courts as evidence); and the damages are infinite and irretrievable by any of the proceedings of our laws.

For the answering all these circumstances, a court might be erected by authority of Parliament, to be composed of six judges commissioners, who should have power to hear and decide as a court of equity, under the title of a "Court Merchant."

The proceedings of this court should be short, the trials speedy, the fees easy, that every man might have immediate remedy where wrong is done. For in trials at law about merchants' affairs the circumstances of the case are often such as the long proceedings of courts of equity are more pernicious than in other cases; because the matters to which they are generally relating are under greater contingencies than in other cases, as effects in hands abroad, which want orders, ships, and seamen lying at demurrage and in pay, and the like.

These six judges should be chosen of the most eminent merchants of the kingdom, to reside in London, and to have power by commission to summon a council of merchants, who should decide all cases on the hearing, of both parties, with appeal to the said judges.

Also to delegate by commission petty councils of merchants in the most considerable ports of the kingdom for the same purpose.

The six judges themselves to be only judges of appeal; all trials to be heard before the council of merchants by methods and proceedings singular and concise.

The council to be sworn to do justice, and to be chosen annually out of the principal merchants of the city.

The proceedings here should be without delay; the plaintiff to exhibit his grievance by way of brief, and the defendant to give in his answer, and a time of hearing to be appointed immediately.

The defendant by motion shall have liberty to put off hearing upon showing good cause, not otherwise.

At hearing, every man to argue his own cause if he pleases, or introduce any person to do it for him.

Attestations and protests from foreign parts, regularly procured and authentically signified in due form, to pass in evidence; affidavits in due form likewise attested and done before proper magistrates within the king's dominions, to be allowed as evidence.

The party grieved may appeal to the six judges, before whom they shall plead by counsel, and from their judgment to have no appeal.

By this method infinite controversies would be avoided and disputes amicably ended, a multitude of present inconveniences avoided, and merchandising matters would in a merchant-like manner be decided by the known customs and methods of trade.

OF SEAMEN.

***

It is observable that whenever this kingdom is engaged in a war with any of its neighbours two great inconveniences constantly follow: one to the king and one to trade.

1. That to the king is, that he is forced to press seamen for the manning of his navy, and force them involuntarily into the service: which way of violently dragging men into the fleet is attended with sundry ill circumstances, as:

(1.) Our naval preparations are retarded, and our fleets always late for want of men, which has exposed them not a little, and been the ruin of many a good and well-laid expedition.

(2.) Several irregularities follow, as the officers taking money to dismiss able seamen, and filling up their complement with raw and improper persons.

(3.) Oppressions, quarrellings, and oftentimes murders, by the rashness of press-masters and the obstinacy of some unwilling to go.

(4.) A secret aversion to the service from a natural principle, common to the English nation, to hate compulsion.

(5.) Kidnapping people out of the kingdom, robbing houses, and picking pockets, frequently practised under pretence of pressing, as has been very much used of late.

With various abuses of the like nature, some to the king, and some to the subject.

2. To trade. By the extravagant price set on wages for seamen, which they impose on the merchant with a sort of authority, and he is obliged to give by reason of the scarcity of men, and that not from a real want of men (for in the height of a press, if a merchantman wanted men, and could get a protection for them, he might have any number immediately, and none without it, so shy were they of the public service).

The first of these things has cost the king above three millions sterling since the war, in these three particulars:

1. Charge of pressing on sea and on shore, and in small craft employed for that purpose.

2. Ships lying in harbour for want of men, at a vast charge of pay and victuals for those they had.

3. Keeping the whole navy in constant pay and provisions all the winter, for fear of losing the men against summer, which has now been done several years, besides bounty money and other expenses to court and oblige the seamen.

The second of these (viz., the great wages paid by the merchant) has cost trade, since the war, above twenty millions sterling. The coal trade gives a specimen of it, who for the first three years of the war gave 9 pounds a voyage to common seamen, who before sailed for 36s.; which, computing the number of ships and men used in the coal trade, and of voyages made, at eight hands to a vessel, does, modestly accounting, make 89,600 pounds difference in one year in wages to seamen in the coal trade only.

For other voyages the difference of sailors' wages is 50s, per month and 55s. per month to foremast-men, who before went for 26s. per month; besides subjecting the merchant to the insolence of the seamen, who are not now to be pleased with any provisions, will admit no half-pay, and command of the captains even what they please; nay, the king himself can hardly please them.

For cure of these inconveniences it is the following project is proposed, with which the seamen can have no reason to be dissatisfied, nor are not at all injured; and yet the damage sustained will be prevented, and an immense sum of money spared, which is now squandered away by the profuseness and luxury of the seamen. For if prodigality weakens the public wealth of the kingdom in general, then are the seamen but ill commonwealths-men, who are not visibly the richer for the prodigious sums of money paid them either by the king or the merchant.

The project is this: that by an Act of Parliament an office or court be erected, within the jurisdiction of the Court of Admiralty, and subject to the Lord High Admiral, or otherwise independent, and subject only to a parliamentary authority, as the commission for taking and stating the public accounts.

In this court or office, or the several branches of it (which, to that end, shall be subdivided and placed in every seaport in the kingdom), shall be listed and entered into immediate pay all the seamen in the kingdom, who shall be divided into colleges or chambers of sundry degrees, suitable to their several capacities, with pay in proportion to their qualities; as boys, youths, servants, men able and raw, midshipmen, officers, pilots, old men, and pensioners.

The circumstantials of this office:

1. No captain or master of any ship or vessel should dare to hire or carry to sea with him any seamen but such as he shall receive from the office aforesaid.

2. No man whatsoever, seaman or other, but applying himself to the said office to be employed as a sailor, should immediately enter into pay, and receive for every able seaman 24s. per month, and juniors in proportion; to receive half-pay while unemployed, and liberty to work for themselves: only to be at call of the office, and leave an account where to be found.

3. No sailor could desert, because no employment would be to be had elsewhere.

4. All ships at their clearing at the Custom House should receive a ticket to the office for men, where would be always choice rather than scarcity, who should be delivered over by the office to the captain or master without any trouble or delay; all liberty of choice to be allowed both to master and men, only so as to give up all disputes to the officers appointed to decide.

> Note. By this would be avoided the great charge captains and owners are at to keep men

on board before they are ready to go; whereas now the care of getting men will be over, and all come on board in one day: for, the captain carrying the ticket to the office, he may go and choose his men if he will; otherwise they will be sent on board to him, by tickets sent to their dwellings to repair on board such a ship.

5. For all these men that the captain or master of the ship takes he shall pay the office, not the seamen, 28s. per month (which 4s. per month overplus of wages will be employed to pay the half-pay to the men out of employ), and so in proportion of wages for juniors.

6. All disputes concerning the mutinying of mariners, or other matters of debate between the captains and men, to be tried by way of appeal in a court for that purpose to be erected, as aforesaid.

7. All discounting of wages and time, all damages of goods, averages, stopping of pay, and the like, to be adjusted by stated and public rules and laws in print, established by the same Act of Parliament, by which means all litigious suits in the Court of Admiralty (which are infinite) would be prevented.

8. No ship that is permitted to enter at the Custom House and take in goods should ever be refused men, or delayed in the delivering them above five days after a demand made and a ticket from the Custom House delivered (general cases, as arrests and embargoes, excepted).

The Consequences of this Method.

1. By this means the public would have no want of seamen, and all the charges and other inconveniences of pressing men would be prevented.

2. The intolerable oppression upon trade, from the exorbitance of wages and insolence of mariners, would be taken off.

3. The following sums of money should be paid to the office, to lie in bank as a public fund for the service of the nation, to be disposed of by order of Parliament, and not otherwise; a committee being a ways substituted in the intervals of the session to audit the accounts, and a treasury for the money, to be composed of members of the House, and to be changed every session of Parliament:

(1). Four shillings per month wages advanced by the merchants to the office for the men, more than the office pays them.

(2). In consideration of the reducing men's wages, and consequently freights, to the former prices (or near them), the owners of ships or merchants shall pay at the importation of all goods forty shillings per ton freight, to be stated upon all goods and ports in proportion; reckoning it on wine tonnage from Canaries as the standard, and on special freights in proportion to the freight formerly paid, and half the said price in times of peace.

Note. – This may well be done, and no burden; for if freights are reduced to their former prices (or near it), as they will be if wages are so too, then the merchant may well pay it: as, for instance, freight from Jamaica to London, formerly at 6 pounds 10s. per ton, now at 18 pounds and 20 pounds; from Virginia, at 5 pounds to 6 pounds 10s., now at 14 pounds, 16 pounds, and 17 pounds; from Barbadoes, at 6 pounds, now at 16 pounds; from Oporto, at 2 pounds, now at 6 pounds; and the like.

The payment of the above-said sums being a large bank for a fund, and it being supposed to be in fair hands and currently managed, the merchants shall further pay upon all goods shipped out, and shipped on board from abroad, for and from any port of this kingdom, 4 pounds per cent. on the real value, bona fide; to be sworn to if demanded. In consideration whereof the said office shall be obliged to pay and make good all losses, damages, averages, and casualties whatsoever, as fully as by the custom of assurances now is done, without any discounts, rebates, or delays whatsoever; the said 4 pounds per cent. to be stated on the voyage to the Barbadoes, and enlarged or taken off, in proportion to the voyage, by rules and laws to be printed and publicly known.

Reserving only, that then, as reason good, the said office shall have power to direct ships of all sorts, how and in what manner, and how long they shall sail with or wait for convoys; and shall have power (with limitations) to lay embargoes on ships, in order to compose fleets for the benefit of convoys.

These rules, formerly noted, to extend to all trading by sea, the coasting and home-fishing trade excepted; and for them it should be ordered–

First, for coals; the colliers being provided with men at 28s. per month, and convoys in sufficient number, and proper stations from Tynemouth Bar to the river, so as they need not go in fleets, but as wind and weather presents, run all the way under the protection of the men-of-war, who should be continually cruising from station to station, they would be able to perform their voyage, in as short time as formerly, and at as cheap pay, and consequently could afford to sell their coals at 17s. per chaldron, as well as formerly at 15s.

Wherefore there should be paid into the treasury appointed at Newcastle, by bond to be paid where they deliver, 10s. per chaldron, Newcastle measure; and the stated price at London to be 27s. per chaldron in the Pool, which is 30s. at the buyer's house; and is so far from being dear, a time of war especially, as it is cheaper than ever was known in a war; and the officers should by proclamation confine the seller to that price.

In consideration also of the charge of convoys, the ships bringing coals shall all pay 1 pound per cent. on the value of the ship, to be agreed on at the office; and all convoy-money exacted by commanders of ships shall be relinquished, and the office to make good all losses of ships, not goods, that shall be lost by enemies only.

These heads, indeed, are such as would need some explication, if the experiment were to be made; and, with submission, would reduce the seamen to better circumstances; at least, it would have them in readiness for any public service much easier than by all the late methods of encouragement by registering seamen,

For by this method all the seamen in the kingdom should be the king's hired servants, and receive their wages from him, whoever employed them; and no man could hire or employ them but from him. The merchant should hire them of the king, and pay the king for them; nor would there be a seaman in England out of employ - which, by the way, would prevent their seeking service abroad. If they were not actually at sea they would receive half-pay, and might be employed in works about the yards, stores, and navy, to keep all things in repair.

If a fleet or squadron was to be fitted out they would be manned in a week's time, for all the seamen in England would be ready. Nor would they be shy of the service; for it is not an aversion to the king's service, nor it is not that the duty is harder in the men-of-war than the Merchantmen, nor it is not fear of danger which makes our seamen lurk and hide and hang back in a time of war, but it is wages is the matter: 24s. per month in the king's service, and 40s. to 50s. per month from the merchant, is the true cause; and the seaman is in the right of it, too; for who would serve his king and country, and fight, and be knocked on the head at 24s. per month that can have 50s. without that hazard? And till this be remedied, in vain are all the encouragements which can be given to seamen; for they tend but to make them insolent, and encourage their extravagance.

Nor would this proceeding be any damage to the seamen in general; for 24s. per month wages, and to be kept in constant service (or half-pay when idle), is really better to the seaman than 45s. per month, as they now take it, considering how long they often lie idle on shore out of pay; for the extravagant price of seamen's wages, though it has been an intolerable burden to trade, has not visibly enriched the sailors, and they may as well be content with 24s. per month now as formerly.

On the other hand, trade would be sensibly revived by it, the intolerable price of freights would be reduced, and the public would reap an immense benefit by the payments mentioned in the proposal; as–

1. 4s. per month upon the wages of all the seamen employed by the merchant (which if we allow 200,000 seamen always in employ, as there cannot be less in all the ships belonging to England) is 40,000 pounds per month.

2. 40s. per ton freight upon all goods imported.

3. 4 per cent. on the value of all goods exported or imported.

4. 10s. per chaldron upon all the coals shipped at Newcastle, and 1 per cent. on the ships which carry them.

What these four articles would pay to the Exchequer yearly it would be very difficult to calculate, and I am too near the end of this book to attempt it: but I believe no tax ever given since this war has come near it.

It is true, out of this the public would be to pay half-pay to the seamen who shall be out of employ, and all the losses, and damages on goods and ships; which, though it might be considerable, would be small, compared to the payment aforesaid: for as the premium of 4 per cent. is but small, so the safety lies upon all men being bound to insure. For I believe any one will grant me this: it is not the smallness of a premium ruins the insurer, but it is the smallness of the quantity he insures; and I am not at all ashamed to affirm that, let but a premium of 4 pounds per cent. be paid into one man's hand for all goods imported and exported, and any man may be the general insurer of the kingdom, and yet that premium can never hurt the merchant either.

So that the vast revenue this would raise would be felt nowhere: neither poor nor rich would pay the more for coals; foreign goods would be brought home cheaper, and our own goods carried to market cheaper; owners would get more by ships, merchants by goods; and losses by sea would be no loss at all to anybody, because repaid by the public stock.

Another unseen advantage would arise by it: we should be able to outwork all our neighbours, even the Dutch themselves, by sailing as cheap and carrying goods as cheap in a time of war as in peace – an advantage which has more in it than is easily thought of, and would have a noble influence upon all our foreign trade. For what could the Dutch do in trade if we could carry our goods to Cadiz at 50s. per ton freight, and they give 8 pounds or 10 pounds and the like in other places? Whereby we could be able to sell cheaper or get more than our neighbours.

There are several considerable clauses might be added to this proposal (some of great advantage to the general trade of the kingdom, some to particular trades, and more to the public), but I avoid being too particular in things which are but the product of my own private opinion.

If the Government should ever proceed to the experiment, no question but much more than has been hinted at would appear; nor do I see any great difficulty in the attempt, or who would be aggrieved at it; and there I leave it, rather wishing than expecting to see it undertaken.

CONCLUSION

Upon a review of the several chapters of this book I find that, instead of being able to go further, some things may have suffered for want of being fully expressed; which if any person object against, I only say, I cannot now avoid it. I have endeavoured to keep to my title, and offered but an essay; which any one is at liberty to go on with as they please, for I can promise no supplement. As to errors of opinion, though I am not yet convinced of any, yet I nowhere pretend to infallibility. However, I do not willingly assert anything which I have not good grounds for. If I am mistaken, let him that finds the error inform the world better, and never trouble himself to animadvert upon this, since I assure him I shall not enter into any pen-and-ink contest on the matter.

As to objections which may lie against any of the proposals made in this book, I have in some places mentioned such as occurred to my thoughts. I shall never assume that arrogance to pretend no other or further objections may be raised; but I do really believe no such objection can be raised as will overthrow any scheme here laid down so as to render the thing impracticable. Neither do I think but that all men will acknowledge most of the proposals in this book would be of as great, and perhaps greater, advantage to the public than I have pretended to.

As for such who read books only to find out the author's faux pas, who will quarrel at the meanness of style, errors of pointing, dulness of expression, or the like, I have but little to say to them. I thought I had corrected it very carefully, and yet some mispointings and small errors have slipped me, which it is too late to help. As to language, I have been rather careful to make it speak English suitable to the manner of the story than to dress it up with exactness of style, choosing rather to have it free and familiar, according to the nature of essays, than to strain at a perfection of language which I rather wish for than pretend to be master of.

Books For ALL Kinds of Readers

At ReadHowYouWant we understand that one size does not fit all types of readers. Our innovative, patent pending technology allows us to design new formats to make reading easier and more enjoyable for you. This helps improve your speed of reading and your comprehension. Our EasyRead printed books have been optimized to improve word recognition, ease eye tracking by adjusting word and line spacing as well as minimizing hyphenation. Our EasyRead SuperLarge editions have been developed to make reading easier and more accessible for vision-impaired readers. We offer Braille and DAISY formats of our books and all popular E-Book formats.

Made in United States
Orlando, FL
04 November 2026

90204188R00118